BOB DYLAN

Brian Southall

THIS IS A CARLTON BOOK
Published in Great Britain in 2015 by
Carlton Books Limited
20 Mortimer Street
London W1T 3JW

Previously published as *Treasures of Bob Dylan* in 2012 by Carlton Books Limited.

Copyright © 2015 Carlton Books Limited

A CIP catalogue record of this book can be obtained from the British Library.

ISBN 978-1-78097-649-5

Printed in China

10 9 8 7 6 5 4 3 2 1

BOB DYLAN

Brian Southall

CARLTON
BOOKS

Contents

Introduction	06
The Early Years	08
New York City	10
The Freewheelin' Bob Dylan and *The Times They Are A-Changin'*	16
Political Dylan	18
Another Side of Bob Dylan	22
Bringing It All Back Home	24
Dylan Goes Electric	26
Highway 61 Revisited	28
Blonde on Blonde	34
"Judas!" The 1966 UK tour	36
John Wesley Harding	40
Nashville Skyline	42
Isle of Wight Festival 1969	46
Self Portrait and *New Morning*	48
Dylan at the Movies	50
Planet Waves and *Before the Flood*	52
Blood on the Tracks and The Rolling Thunder Revue	54
Desire, *Hard Rain* and *Street Legal*	58
The Gospel Years	62
The Wilderness Years	66
Oh Mercy	70
Into the 1990s	74
A Return to Form	78
Love and Theft and *Modern Times*	80
Together Through Life and *Christmas in the Heart*	84
The Never Ending Tour	86

"I don't care to define what I do."

Bob Dylan

Introduction by Brian Southall

It seems appropriate that as part of an introduction, I should mention how Bob Dylan first came into my life. As with for so many other British teenagers in the heady days of the 1960s, it was through his second album *The Freewheelin' Bob Dylan* and its peace anthems and protest songs. I bought it, played it incessantly and also studied the front cover photo of Bob and his girlfriend walking arm-in-arm down a snow-covered street in New York. That was in 1963, and in February 1977 when I first visited New York (I was head of press at EMI and there with Queen) the journalist Mick Brown took me to the very same street to pay homage to the spirit of Bob Dylan ... and magically it was still covered in six inches of snow.

RIGHT Bob Dylan toured the UK in 1965 with his trademark acoustic guitar and harmonica.

Earlier, when I was a journalist on a local newspaper, I went along to see Dylan at London's Royal Albert Hall. It was 1965 – the year before he went 'electric' – and for reasons known only to my editor, I was allowed to review the concert ... and claim the rail fare on expenses.

I told my readers that "he showed great talent and that not everybody needs a full orchestral backing or an electric guitar" and that he entertained a packed house with "just plain talent and originality." In my maddest moments I like to think that maybe I played a small part in ensuring that his career would run on for another five decades!

My affection has continued to the present day although I now accept that he is entitled to use an electric guitar if he wants to and I also know that his live shows are as likely to be a disappointment as they are a joy. Earls Court in 1978 was one of the joyous moments while London Docklands Arena in 2002 was ... let's just say we left early!

The Beatles' love and respect for Dylan has been well documented and while one writer suggested that "Without Bob Dylan rock 'n' roll as we know it would not exist," another described him as "The most influential folk/rock vocalist/composer ever." On the other hand, those who have worked on releasing and promoting his albums have occasionally taken a different view.

One CBS executive who spent time backstage waving the corporate flag during Dylan's visits to the UK recounts, "He really couldn't give a toss about whether we turned up or not. He's not remotely interested." While the same man acknowledges the genius of Bob Dylan, he also retains a vivid recollection of his meetings with the great man. "He was never charming and was basically a curmudgeonly old fuck."

Walter Yetnikoff, the man who ran CBS in America, was another

executive who saw the unhelpful and unresponsive side of Dylan but he never let it bother him. "If he wanted to sulk in the corner, let him sulk in the corner," was his philosophy.

At the same time, multi-million selling singer Mick Hucknall acknowledges the value of Dylan's simplistic attitude to the music business. "He has enhanced his image as the wandering troubadour by just touring, playing and recording and not really bothering about the media."

The story goes that when former Bananarama and Shakespeare's Sister singer Siobhan Fahey was married to Dave Stewart, Dylan joined them for dinner one night. During the evening Dylan contributed almost nothing to the conversation and when Mrs Stewart asked her husband, "What do you think is going on in there?" the former Eurythmics star said simply, "Everything."

Bob Dylan is undoubtedly an enigmatic genius and he has perhaps deliberately created an aura of indifference and even rudeness in order to keep away those aspects of fame and success which he considers unnecessary, skittish and wearisome.

British guitarist Mick Ronson joined Dylan's Rolling Thunder tour in 1975 and told people he was convinced that Dylan never knew his name and insisted on referring to him – both on and off stage – as simply "the Limey."

On the other hand Bob Dylan does have an interest in everyday things such as shopping and recreation. My only close encounter with him took place on the street in London's Mayfair in 1978, when he was on his way to an up-market clothes shop.

He was with CBS press officer Elly Smith and I made my way over in order to meet her escort. I said hello – there was no handshake – and for the next five or six minutes I rambled on about the impact Dylan and his music had had on me and how I was looking forward to seeing him on stage. While I spoke, and

Elly chipped in with some observations, Dylan said nothing ... absolutely nothing, not even goodbye!

Ms Smith was also the person who had to arrange a spot of physical recreation for Dylan during that 1978 visit. His hotel didn't have a pool so she called up a larger five-star hotel to ask if Mr. Dylan could come down for a dip. "He didn't want the pool cleared or anything but I did ask for a time when it might be quiet," she recalls. "We got there and went into the pool which was completely empty except for all the cleaning staff who were standing on the side with their mops and brooms just watching Bob Dylan swim."

For another former record company executive it was time spent with Alice Cooper in 1991 which yielded an unexpected Dylan moment. "I arranged to play golf with Alice at Wentworth and he said he was going to bring a friend," explains Paul Russell. "I told him I needed to know his name a day or so before and when Alice called, he said he was bringing Bob Dylan." Russell got another CBS artist to make up a foursome – "a Welsh guy who was so gobsmacked to be playing with Alice Cooper and Bob Dylan that he couldn't hit a ball all day" – and gave his two most famous guests their dress code. "I told them they had to wear golf hats and no trainers were allowed in the club house and they turned up with all the right clothing and equipment but we sat outside. They both kept their caps on and nobody recognized them. Bob took it very seriously and played very well, although Alice won."

Singer, songwriter, performer, protester, swimmer and golfer – you can choose your own Bob Dylan image. For me he remains one of the few genuinely inspirational artists ever to enter the world of popular music ... even if he did ignore me. But then I'd forgive him everything for just a handful of his songs which have thankfully found their way into my life.

The Early Years

Though now more than 70, Bob Dylan has never lost his simple yearning to make music, though fame, fortune and commerciality sometimes threatened to dam the pure stream of his creativity: a stream that rose in his formative years, in what was, prior to the addition of Alaska, America's most northerly state.

Robert Allen Zimmerman was born on May 24, 1941, in the Midwestern town of Duluth, Minnesota, and from the age of six was raised in the nearby town of Hibbing, a once prosperous iron mining community close to Lake Superior. Water plays a big part in Minnesota's history; the state, which borders mainland Canada, takes its name from a Native American word meaning "Land of a thousand lakes."

Although he was born seven months before America entered World War Two, following the Japanese bombing of Pearl Harbor, Dylan once reflected on what it meant to come into the world in the midst of warfare and with the threat of invasion hanging in the air: "If you were born around that time or were living and alive, you could feel the old world go and the new one beginning."

At school, many of his teachers were the same people who had taught his mother and, as Dylan approached his teenage years, the Cold War and the Iron Curtain focused American fears on the threat of a Russian invasion, which according to Dylan was a genuine fear in his home state. "The Reds were everywhere – we were told – and out for blood lust," he said.

Growing up, Dylan discovered the radio – a passion he would return to for this *Theme Time Hour* sessions in 2006 – and quickly became fascinated by blues and country music before becoming engrossed, in the mid-1950s, by the fast-emerging phenomenon that was rock 'n' roll. From listening to records on the radio the young Dylan turned to playing music live and his earliest attempts were with bands called The Jokers (formed in a Jewish summer camp), The Show Boaters and The Golden Chords.

Schoolwork regularly took a back seat as the young Zimmerman took off to go on the road as a carny ("I was with the carnival on and off for six years"), where he worked on rides such as the Ferris wheel. "I didn't go to school for a bunch of years," he admitted, before adding: "It all came out even, though." He eventually graduated from Hibbing High School aged 18, just a few months after he'd seen Buddy Holly perform in Duluth. Five days after the show at the town's National Guard Armory, Holly died in a plane crash in neighbouring Iowa, aged just 22.

ABOVE Dylan's home in Seventh Avenue, Hibbing, Minnesota, which has been renamed Bob Dylan Drive.

The young Dylan was a fan of the bespectacled Texan, but soon moved on to discover the Everly Brothers before returning to the one performer who, for him, stood head and shoulders above all others. The youngster who called himself Bobby Zimmerman had discovered Richard Penniman and the joys of 'Tutti Frutti' and 'Lucille'." So impressed was Zimmerman that his 1959 high school yearbook entry lists his ambition as "to follow Little Richard."

Another major turning-point came in the same year when Zimmerman, who had taken to calling himself Elston Gunn, made his way to Fargo in nearby North Dakota and made contact with local act Bobby Vee and the Shadows. He talked himself into a job as a backing pianist on a few local shows, for a total of $30, but when he got back home he bragged that he'd actually played piano on Vee's US Top 100 hit 'Suzie Baby', even though it was recorded before he joined the band. Those locals familiar with young Master Gunn soon came to realize that he would often change names and confuse fact and fiction when he recounted his experiences.

It was time to stretch his wings, and Zimmerman left for the city of Minneapolis, and Minnesota State University. It was here that he began to move away from rock 'n' roll and focus his attention on his country's folk music. "I knew that when I got into folk music, it was a more serious type of thing," he explained later. "The songs are

ABOVE A postcard from Hibbing giving pride of place to the town's (and Bob Dylan's) High School.

filled with more despair, more sadness, more triumphs, more faith in the supernatural, much deeper feelings."

Fuelled by his new-found love of folk, and the music of artists such as Woody Guthrie, Pete Seeger, Odetta and Dave Van Ronk, Gunn/Zimmerman began to appear on Minneapolis' folk circuit, in the Dinkytown district close to the university. And here a new name began to emerge.

"You call yourself what you want to call yourself," he explained. "This is the land of the free." So Robert Zimmerman, now Elston Gunn, toyed with becoming Robert Allen or Robert Alleyn, while rejecting both Robert Dylan and Bobby Dylan – stories say the new surname was inspired by either the Welsh poet Dylan Thomas, a distant relation named Dillon or even the American TV lawman Marshal Matt Dillon – in favour of Bob Dylan. At one point Dylan contemplated Woody as a first name in honour of his new-found hero Woody Guthrie, whose songs, such as 'This Land Is Your Land', 'Tom Joad' and 'Grand Coulee Dam', he enthusiastically added to his list of titles as he learnt to master the guitar and harmonica. It was his determination to meet the Oklahoma-born sometime hobo and regular busking musician Guthrie that convinced Dylan to leave Minnesota and make his way east to New Jersey and New York City.

RIGHT Dylan was inspired to play the harmonica by folk singer and protester Woody Guthrie.

New York City

Bob Dylan was so in thrall to the music – the cause of America's poor and the legend that was Woodrow Wilson Guthrie – that in late 1960 he travelled close to 1,500 miles to meet him.

Perhaps in tribute to the man who himself crisscrossed America riding free in railway boxcars, Dylan even told people he journeyed from Minnesota to New York on a freight train, although he later admitted: "What I did was come across country from the Midwest in a four-door sedan, '57 Impala." Making his way to New York was all about music: "I was here to find singers, the ones I'd heard on record – but most of all to find Woody Guthrie."

Dylan arrived in New York in late January 1961 and within a few days was at the Greystone Park Hospital in New Jersey where Guthrie, 48, was being treated for Huntington's chorea, a hereditary disease that had killed his mother. There Dylan chatted with and even sang to his hero before leaving with the inspiration to write a song. 'Song To Woody' was, according to Dylan, "the first song I ever wrote that I performed in public."

New York's Greenwich Village offered the young man from Minnesota every opportunity to develop his art and pursue his dream. In clubs, bars and coffee houses such as Café Wha?, The Gaslight, Gerde's Folk City and The Kettle of Fish, Dylan saw and met the people he had come to find – Dave Van Ronk, Richie Havens, Josh White, Brownie McGhee and Sonny Terry and the Seegers – Pete, Peggy and Mike.

Playing afternoon gigs for a dollar and a cheeseburger, Dylan

LEFT Dylan accompanies Karen Dalton and Fred Neil in the Café Wha? in 1961.

ABOVE The hugely influential Woody Guthrie with his famous 'Fascists' guitar entertains his fellow travellers on the New York subway.

began to forge a path in New York's Bohemian hotspot. He supported John Lee Hooker and played harmonica on sessions for Harry Belafonte before a Folk City show in September 1961, where he was seen and praised by influential *New York Times* music critic Robert Shelton. The review caught the eye of legendary CBS/Columbia producer and talent scout John Hammond who, after hiring Dylan to accompany singer Carolyn Hester, offered him a recording contract. Hammond's involvement with the likes of Billie Holiday, Count Basie, Bessie Smith and Benny Goodman was well known to Dylan, who put pen to paper without a second glance: "I would have gladly signed whatever form he put in front of me."

As he prepared to go into the studio, Dylan played a showcase at New York's celebrated Carnegie Chapter Hall to an audience of just 53. Undeterred, he and Hammond recorded *Bob Dylan* in just two days, November 20 and 22, 1961. As yet without a portfolio of his own songs, Dylan was obliged to search for material for his eponymous debut release. Time spent in the folk clubs of New York had opened his ears to a wide selection of authentic traditional music, and he opted to arrange four of the final 13 songs himself.

'In My Time Of Dyin'', 'Man Of Constant Sorrow', 'Pretty Peggy-O' and 'Gospel Plow' joined Dave Van Ronk's arrangement of 'House Of The Rising Sun', Roy Acuff's treatment of 'Freight Train Blues' and Eric Von Schmidt's arrangement of 'Baby Let Me Follow You Down' alongside Jesse Fuller's 'You're No Good', Bukka White's 'Fixin' To Die', Curtis Jones' 'Highway 51' and 'See That My Grave Is Kept Clean' by Blind Lemon Jefferson, to create the bulk of the album.

To complete his debut Dylan added two of his own songs, 'Talkin' New York Blues' and his tribute 'Song To Woody'. Four other songs – 'House Carpenter', 'He Was A Friend Of Mine' and Guthrie's 'Ramblin' Man Blues', plus Dylan's third original song from the period, 'Man On The Street' – missed the final track selection.

According to Hammond, his new find was somewhat less than the perfect recording artist; besides problems with his enunciation of the letters P and S, Dylan regularly wandered "off mic,"

In March 1962, *Bob Dylan* hit the shops, while the accompanying first single, 'Mixed Up Confusion', hit the airwaves. Neither album nor single, which was swiftly withdrawn by Columbia, made the US charts (the album did peak at number 13 in the UK three years on), but they did create a stir around the city's folk circuit where Dylan's shows were becoming a major draw.

Before the year was out Dylan decided to change his name legally to Bob Dylan, while at the same time signing a management deal with Albert Grossman. Of those two decisions one would last the rest of the decade, the other a lifetime.

ABOVE Some very rare, bootleg examples of Dylan's earliest known (1960s) recordings.

RIGHT Dylan pauses for thought during his debut recording sessions for Columbia

Bob Dylan
Released March 1962. Tracks: You're No Good / Talkin' New York Blues / In My Time Of Dyin' / Man Of Constant Sorrow Fixin' To Die / Pretty Peggy-O / Highway 51 / Gospel Plow / Baby Let Me Follow You Down / House Of the Rising Sun / Freight Train Blues / Song To Woody / See That My Grave Is Kept Clean

FIRST NEW YORK APPEARANCE   4-11-61   BOB DYLAN

FOLK CiTY   130 West 3rd St. (at 6th Ave.) N.Y.C.   © 1978

"I'm only 21 years old and I know that there's been too many wars ... you people over 21 should know better."

Bob Dylan, on composing 'Blowin' in the Wind'

LEFT Poster from Bob Dylan's first appearance in New York City, April 11, 1961 at Folk City.

Bob DYLAN
DEC. 5
IN CONCERT-8:30 P.M
WILSON HI. SCHOOL

8:30 P.M.	Ticket Prices	Harbor Guitar	Benaderet Music Co.
Wilson Hi. Sch.	$4.00	Newport Blvd.	E. 1st Street
4400 E. 10th. St.	$3.00	Costa Mesa	Long Beach
in Long Beach	$2.00		

For information,	You may buy	McCabe's Guitar shops	send Check or Money
contact the	Tickets at the	E. Anaheim	order to The
Golden Bear.	following places.	Long Beach	Golden Bear
phone 536 9600		Pico Blvd. Santa Monica	Ocean Ave. hwy. Huntington Beach
		Melrose Hollywood	

PRESENTED BY THE GOLDEN BEAR

ABOVE Bob Dylan sticker.

RIGHT Flyer from the Wilson High
School concert, December 5, 1964.

gerdes
FOLK CITY
new york's center of folk music
HELD OVER BY POPULAR DEMAND
THRU   APRIL 23
John Lee Hooker
COUNTRY BLUES SINGER
and
BOB DYLAN

SHOW BEGINNING 9:30.

11 W. 4th STREET - AL 4-8449   NEVER A
                                     COVER CHARGE
I BLOCK WEST OF B'WAY
EVERY MONDAY - HOOTENANNY 8 GUEST NIGHT

open every night

LEFT On the bill as support for John Lee Hooker in April 1961.

RIGHT Dylan playing in Mississippi in 1963 at a black voter rally.

The Freewheelin' Bob Dylan
and *The Times They Are A-Changin'*

In December 1962 Dylan travelled to Britain for the first time at the invitation of TV director Philip Saville, who had seen him perform in Greenwich Village. He had Dylan in mind for the role of Bobby the Hobo in a TV play called *Madhouse On Castle Street.*

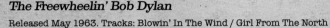

The Freewheelin' Bob Dylan

Released May 1963. Tracks: Blowin' In The Wind / Girl From The North Country / Masters Of War / Down the Highway / Bob Dylan's Blues / A Hard Rain's A-Gonna Fall / Don't Think Twice It's Alright / Bob Dylan's Dream / Oxford Town / Talking World War III Blues / Corinna Corinna / Honey Just Allow Me One More Chance / I Shall Be Free.

While in London Dylan sang in folk clubs and pubs such as the Troubadour, Bunjies, Les Cousins and the King And Queen and in January, during his last week in England, he went into the studio to supply backing vocals on an album by Dick Farina and Eric Von Schmidt – credited as Blind Boy Grunt. His trip also brought him into contact with traditional British songs such as 'Scarborough Fair' and 'Lady Franklin's Lament', which would stay with him when he began work on his second album.

As recording got under way, manager Grossman attempted to have Hammond replaced as Dylan's producer but, despite major differences of opinion and attitude, Hammond stayed, although jazz producer Tom Wilson joined the project.

Recording began in April and the album was completed a year later, in April 1963, with 11 songs credited as Dylan compositions; he was emerging as the creator of his own music, with an eye towards social change.

There are many stand-out tracks on the album that would appear in May 1963 as *The Freewheelin' Bob Dylan*, with Don Hunstein's evocative cover shot of Dylan and girlfriend Suze Rotolo walking near their apartment on West 4th Street.

'Blowin' In The Wind' was written in The Commons, a Greenwich coffee house, in April 1962. Seen as a universal protest song for a new generation, he explained it thus: "I'm only 21 years old and I know that there's been too many wars … you people over 21 should know better." It was the first Dylan song to make it into the charts, when folk trio Peter, Paul and Mary (also managed by Grossman) took it into the top 10 in both the US and the UK.

'Girl From The North Country,' first conceived back in the late 1950s, was eventually completed with 'Scarborough Fair' as its basis. He wrote the lyrics down in late 1962 and finished it in Italy the following January.

'A Hard Rain's A-Gonna Fall' began as a long free verse poem and,

thanks in part to the Cuban missile crisis of 1962, became a youth anthem. While denying the "hard rain" was nuclear fallout, Dylan said: "I don't really care to define what I do."

'Don't Think Twice It's Alright' was one of his earliest love songs, inspired by Rotolo, but was taken into the American Top 10 by Peter, Paul and Mary in 1963 and into the British Top 10 by Dylan himself in 1965. Dylan's next girlfriend, singer Joan Baez, performed it in 1963 and, referring to Rotolo, announced it as a song "about a love affair that has lasted too long."

The album brought Dylan his first real taste of commercial success when it went gold in America and reached number 22 in the US charts. In the UK it would top the charts for two weeks in April 1965.

August 1963 saw Dylan back in Columbia's Studio A in New York, and this time Wilson was the sole producer in charge of recording the 11 new songs delivered by Dylan, by now a popular and influential figure – even if Wilson started with some reservations. "I didn't particularly like folk music. I thought folk music was for dumb old guys. This guy played like the dumb guys. But then these words came out!"

Prophetically entitled *The Times They Are A-Changin'*, it was recorded between August and October and focused on the major issues affecting America and the world – racism, poverty and injustice. The title track – once described as "a battle hymn for a generation" – was completed in the last week of recording and was Dylan's first UK single release in the spring of 1965. *Melody Maker* reviewer Ray Coleman told his readers that Dylan was "more a commentator than a singer," before adding, "You can't dance to it. But you CAN think to it." The single – described by Dylan as: "A song with a purpose. I wanted to write a big song: some kind of theme song" – hit the UK Top 10.

'With God On Our Side' was completed on the second day – August 7, 1963 – and joined the track listing as one of the decade's starkest protest anthems.

ABOVE Cigarette in hand, Dylan poses for the camera.

RIGHT Bob Dylan and Joan Baez – they were partners both on and off stage.

'One Too Many Mornings' was the most personal song in a collection made up mainly of protest tracks; and it described the end of his relationship with Rotolo. It was recorded during the same session as the title track. His by then former girlfriend also inspired the song 'Boots Of Spanish Leather'.

'The Lonesome Death Of Hattie Carroll', one of Dylan's earliest reportage songs, focuses on an event in Baltimore on February 9, 1963, when black waitress Carroll, a mother of 11, died of a brain haemorrhage attributed to stress following a drunken assault by wealthy, spoilt local 24-year-old William Zantzinger. He stood trial for murder but was found guilty of manslaughter and sentenced to six months in prison.

Released in January 1964, in the aftermath of John F Kennedy's assassination and Martin Luther King's "I have a dream" speech, the album reached number 20 in America, but would eventually, in April 1965, hit number 4 in the UK.

The Times They Are A-Changin'

Released January 1964. Tracks: The Times They Are A-Changin' / Ballad Of Hollis Brown / With God On Our Side / One Too Many Mornings / North Country Blues / Only A Pawn In Their Game / Boots Of Spanish Leather / When The Ship Comes In / The Lonesome Death Of Hattie Carroll / Restless Farewell

Political Dylan

Dylan and politics were never far apart as he consistently strove to make his voice heard, and in May 1963 – just as his debut album was being released across America – he made his first very public stand against authority, taking as his inspiration earlier musicians with a conscience and a message, including Woody Guthrie, Pete Seeger and Odetta.

Invited on to the hugely influential primetime *Ed Sullivan Show* – produced by the television arm of his record company, CBS – Dylan was all set to sing 'Talkin' John Birch Paranoid Blues' when a station executive suggested he perform another song for fear of libelling the John Birch Society, a radical right-wing political group strongly opposed to communism and civil rights and named after a Baptist missionary and US intelligence officer shot by communists in China in 1945. Dylan would not agree to the censorship and refused to appear on the show, which led to reports in the New York Times, Billboard and Village Voice. The song itself had been recorded for inclusion on Dylan's debut album *The Freewheelin' Bob Dylan* but was cut at some stage, although there is no hard evidence this was done as a direct result of the TV show incident.

Fresh from his dispute with CBS TV, Dylan flew south to Mississippi to join Pete Seeger at a black voter registration rally in the aftermath of the murder of black civil rights organizer Medgar Evers. There in Greenwood he sang the song 'Only A Pawn In Their Game' for the first time.

Alongside fellow-singer and protester Joan Baez, Dylan continued to champion the burgeoning civil rights movement and they both song 'With God On Our Side' at the 1963 Newport Folk Festival before joining the momentous March to Washington in August 1963 when 200,000 people – led by Martin Luther King – gathered to protest for jobs, justice and peace. Dylan performed 'Blowin' In the Wind' and left America's capital city as "the voice of a generation."

These events were very much the inspiration for Dylan's outpouring on his album *The Times They Are A-Changin'*, although he did declare in 1963: "I don't think what comes out of my music is a call to action," and added a couple of years later: "Songs aren't going to save the world." Whether he was right or not, it was a fact that the music of Bob Dylan was now playing a major role in shaping the thoughts and actions of people all around the globe.

With the assassination of President Kennedy in November 1963, the chances of someone taking a pot-shot at Dylan began to increase. In response, he made a point of reiterating that he wasn't a protest singer and made himself less available and less visible, hoping he wouldn't be singled out as the supposed spokesman for white, middle-class activists and protesters.

Though still shaken by Kennedy's murder, the following month Dylan agreed to accept the Tom Paine Award at the annual Bill of Rights dinner in Washington. Given in honour of English-born author, pamphleteer, radical and intellectual Thomas Paine, who emigrated to America in 1774 to become one of the Founding Fathers of the United States, the award had gone to philosopher Bertrand Russell in 1962.

Uncomfortable, and perhaps even regretting having attended, Dylan got drunk and turned on the organizers, the Emergency Civil Liberties Committee, questioning their role and their members. He was booed and hissed, and later apologized for his actions via a prose poem, but he wasn't finished, and later suggested that the audience that night "had nothing to do with my kind of politics."

Dylan's political passion lay in bringing injustice, warmongering, poverty and racism to the forefront of mainstream America's consciousness. He'd done it through songs about the killing of Hattie Carroll and Medgar Evers and also in 'The Death of Emmett Till', a black man murdered in Mississippi in 1955, while in 'With God On Our Side', 'Masters Of War' and 'A Hard Rain's A-Gonna Fall' he made clear his feelings about weapons and the military and, with 'The Times They Are A-Changin'' and 'Talkin' John Birch Paranoid Blues', he took his stand in favour of civil rights.

But by the end of 1963 Dylan stood at a crossroads, and there were those who believed things were about to change, as they spotted signs that Dylan was losing patience with the increasing organization of the protest movement.

Bobby Dylan

ABOVE A rare picture disk album of bootleg Dylan tunes from the mid- to late 1960s.

RIGHT Bob Dylan, Joan Baez and Paul Stookey perform in front at the Lincoln Memorial in 1963.

OVERLEAF In front of the camera before refusing to appear on *The Ed Sullivan Show*.

Another Side Of Bob Dylan

The next album, his fourth in as many years, was to be the first in a series that showed Dylan in a new, softer and more personal light. Aptly entitled *Another Side Of Bob Dylan*, it drew criticism from the folk community who sensed they might be losing their main man. Accused of being caught up with fame and out of touch with the times, Dylan did appear to be relinquishing his mantle as spokesman for America's angry youth, confirming to New Yorker magazine that "there ain't any finger-pointin' songs" on his new album.

He wrote some of the songs during a three-week road trip across America with friends Paul Clayton, Victor Maymudes and Pete Jarman in February 1964. They drove south from New York to visit first New Orleans, then Dallas, where they saw the spot where Kennedy had been shot, before turning west to head for Los Angeles and San Francisco.

According to Dylan the trip was about "talking to people – that's where it's at, man," but he also found time, seated in the back seat of the station-wagon with his typewriter, to create both songs and poetry.

In May, before recording began, Dylan briefly crossed the Atlantic for his first major British concert, at the Royal Festival Hall. The trip also served to promote the three albums already in his catalogue, and Dylan was interviewed by a select few British journalists. One, from *New Musical Express*, got an insight into Dylan's style of songwriting: "The words come first. Then I fit a tune or just strum the chords. Really, I'm no tune-writer. The songs for me are very confining, or something." Asked about the idea of British singers performing blues, soul or American folk, Dylan said: "If an English singer's happy singing a Southern US ballad, I'd rather see him being happy than see him doing something else and being unhappy."

For the show, on Sunday, May 17, Dylan opted to sing 18 of his own songs, although there remains some mystery over the final set

ABOVE A pensive Dylan takes a break (**ABOVE RIGHT**), before adopting a far away look for a more posed shot.

list. The Performing Right Society form shows three tracks listed only as "new song", and it's possible these were previously unheard tracks from his forthcoming album.

From London, Dylan travelled to Paris, where he met a German model named Christa Paffgen, who was later to find fame with The Velvet Underground as Nico. While they were together in Greece, Dylan put the finishing touches to many of the songs destined for the album.

Back in New York, Columbia quickly allocated him studio time with producer Tom Wilson and, astonishingly, he finished the album in a single day. In fact, in just one session, in Studio A on June 9, 1964, during which Dylan drank two bottles of Beaujolais, recorded 14 original songs and selected 11 for *Another Side Of Bob Dylan*. Being organized, it seems, was a key part of his recording process, as Wilson observed: "He always had his songs written out when he came into the studio."

'All I Really Want To Do', completed after returning from Europe, was one of Dylan's most lighthearted songs and was taken into the UK Top five by The Byrds, while in America Cher's version made the top 20.

The symbolic 'Black Crow Blues' was also completed in New York; with Dylan adding piano to his familiar guitar and harmonica. It was completed alongside 'Spanish Harlem Incident', a story of new romance featuring some of the writer's most unusual word couplings.

'Chimes Of Freedom' was written during Dylan's road trip after meeting civil rights activists Cordell Reagon and Bernice Johnson in Atlanta. His lyrics reflect the writer's new-found muse, French poet Arthur Rimbaud.

'My Back Pages' was the last track recorded during the mammoth one-day session, which ended at 1.30am, and contains some of Dylan's finest lyrics including the reflective line about his life so far: "I was so much older then, I'm younger than that now."

'To Ramona' was written in Greece, though about whom remains a topic for debate; one interpretation is that the subject is Joan Baez, and that the song makes reference to her desire to remain part of the folk movement Dylan had rejected.

'Ballad In Plain D' describes his parting from Suze Rotolo in 1964, partly as a result of his relationship with Baez. One of Dylan's most vicious, self-pitying songs, some critics have suggested it should have been left off the album, or never recorded at all.

'It Ain't Me Babe' again focuses on the break-up of his relationship with Rotolo and may have been written while they were apart during Dylan's brief UK tour in March 1964. The Turtles took the song into the US top 10 in 1965, while Johnny Cash hit the US top 30 with it in the same year.

It may have been Dylan himself who decided it would be the final track on what would be his last acoustic album, although producer Wilson saw a new opportunity: "I said if you put some background to this you might have a white Ray Charles with a message." Perhaps reflecting the less protest-orientated nature of the album, *Another Side Of Bob Dylan* edged into the US top 50 during 1964 while in the UK, on the back of his debut show, it reached number eight.

Another Side Of Bob Dylan
Released August 1964. Tracks: All I Really Want To Do / Black Crow Blues / Spanish Harlem Incident / Chimes Of Freedom / I Shall Be Free #10 / To Ramona / Motorpsycho Nightmare / My Back Pages / I Don't Believe You / Ballad In Plain D / It Ain't Me Babe

LEFT A poster advertising Dylan as top of the bill in New York's Philharmonic Hall on Hallowe'en Night in 1964.

ABOVE With four albums under his belt, Dylan was playing to sellout concerts on both sides of the Atlantic Ocean.

Bringing It All Back Home

By the time *Another Side Of Bob Dylan* was finished, Dylan knew he had to move on from his accepted role as a protest singer.

Most of summer 1964 was spent in Woodstock in upstate New York, where Grossman had a house. August's visitors included Joan Baez, who noted: "Most of the month or so we were there Dylan stood at the typewriter in the corner of his room, drinking red wine and smoking and typing away relentlessly for hours."

He was engrossed in writing his next album, an unexpected, controversial fusion of folk and rock created with producer Wilson. The man who had worked on all Dylan's previous albums then predicted things would change for him. "But it wasn't until later that everyone agreed that we should put a band behind him. I had to find a band. But it was a very gradual process." Dylan had first experienced the fusion of folk and rock in the work of John P. Hammond, son of the man who signed him to Columbia, when he was working with three members of The Hawks.

Nonetheless, when Dylan began work on the album on June 13, 1965, it was still as an acoustic artist, playing piano and guitar on ten tracks with Wilson at the controls; however, none was destined to make it on to the new release. The following day, the band Wilson

had assembled – guitarists Al Gorgoni, Kenneth Rankin and Bruce Langhorne, pianist Paul Griffin, bass players Joseph Macho Jnr. and William Lee, plus drummer Bobby Gregg – turned up to play on eight new songs. As usual, they were completed in just a few takes, and included 'Subterranean Homesick Blues', 'Love Minus Zero' and 'She Belongs To Me'.

After a break, Hammond Jnr and The Lovin' Spoonful's John Sebastian joined Langhorne and Dylan in an evening session which produced unacceptable versions of six songs, but the next day it was back on course, with Frank Owens taking over on piano. They worked through tracks including 'Maggie's Farm', 'Gates Of Eden', 'It's All Over Now Baby Blue' and 'Mr. Tambourine Man', although this song, then featuring Ramblin' Jack Elliot, had been taped but rejected in 1964.

The product of three days' recording would be *Bringing It All Back Home* which, despite Dylan recording rock versions of almost every song, appeared in March 1965 with an electric side and a four-song acoustic side featuring Langhorne's balanced guitar accompaniment.

Opener 'Subterranean Homesick Blues' was, for many, the first example of Dylan's move from folk to rock. Written in the New York apartment of his manager's assistant, it tips its hat to Woody Guthrie's 'Taking It Easy' and could be called one of the earliest examples of rap, with its rapid-fire delivery and R&B feel. It would become Dylan's first US chart single, peaking at number 39, and his second UK top 10 hit.

'She Belongs To Me' clearly refers to folk singer, fellow-protester and sometime girlfriend Baez by mentioning an Egyptian ring Dylan had given her. Recorded at the first session on June 13, it was reworked the following day when the electric band assembled in Columbia's Studio B.

'Maggie's Farm' was finished in one take during the final June 15 session; fast-paced and slightly rambling, it also became a UK top 30 hit.

'Love Minus Zero' was one of five songs recorded in three-and-a-half hours with the full band on June 15. Guitarist Langhorne, who also played with Baez, Gordon Lightfoot, Tom Rush and Buffy St Marie, recalled: "We just did first takes … it was amazingly intuitive and successful."

'Mr. Tambourine Man', opening the album's acoustic side, was saved from his previous LP while Dylan perfected it in live performances in the months before these sessions. Written in New Orleans and completed in New Jersey, some consider its lyrics inspired by marijuana while others suggest its title came from the huge tambourine Langhorne played on live dates; recorded by The Byrds, it brought the Los Angeles band a number one hit in both the US and the UK.

This was also the song which introduced a young Mick Hucknall to Bob Dylan. Although he was only five, the leader of Simply Red was impressed by both the song and Dylan's look. "He seemed like the first guy I'd seen just standing there with an acoustic guitar and a mouth organ. 'Mr Tambourine Man' grabbed my attention because of that look but also through the lyrics; I visualized the lyrics and that really captured my imagination."

'It's Alright Ma (I'm Only Bleeding)' was recorded in a single take on the final day of recording and serves as a powerful reminder of Dylan's prowess as a protest singer and his ability to perform 'live' in the studio.

Dylan's fifth studio album closed with fourth acoustic track 'It's All Over Now Baby Blue' inspired, he said, by Gene Vincent's 'Baby Blue' which he sang in his school band days. Seen by some as Dylan's farewell to his earlier self, it earned Baez a UK top 30 hit.

Bringing It All Back Home, featuring Grossman's wife Sally and Dylan's cat Rolling Stone on the cover, became his first US top 10 album and his second UK number one.

Bringing It All Back Home
Released March 1965. Tracks: Subterranean Homesick Blues / She Belongs To Me / Maggie's Farm / Love Minus Zero Outlaw Blues / On The Road Again / Bob Dylan's 115th Dream / Mr. Tambourine Man / Gates Of Eden / It's Alright Ma (I'm Only Bleeding) / It's All Over Now Baby Blue

FAR LEFT Sharing a ride with Ramblin' Jack Elliott.

LEFT Dylan offers up a harmonica solo in the studio.

RIGHT One of Dylan's early solo recording sessions in the CBS studios in New York.

Dylan Goes Electric

It was in 1963 when The Beatles first got to grips with the music of Bob Dylan. According to lead guitarist George Harrison, when they embarked on a three-week stint at the Olympia theatre in Paris, "one of the most memorable things for me was that we had a copy of Bob Dylan's *Freewheelin'* album which we played constantly".

John Lennon also recalled the visit to France as pivotal in their exposure to America's newest sensation: "I think that was the first time I ever heard Dylan at all. We all went potty on Dylan."

They met the following year when he visited the group's hotel twice during their second visit to New York in August 1964, and he unquestionably had a profound effect on the songwriting of Lennon and Paul McCartney.

It was in New York's Delmonico Hotel that Dylan also introduced the four boys from Liverpool to marijuana, wrongly believing they were already familiar with the drug; he had misheard the line "I can't hide" in 'I Want To Hold Your Hand' as "I get high." During what Paul described as a "crazy party," Britain's leading group and America's finest singer-songwriter "got on very well and we just talked and had a big laugh," according to Paul.

Lennon later acknowledged that his song 'I'm A Loser' was inspired by Dylan and added, "Anyone who's one of the best in his field – as Dylan is – is bound to influence people. I wouldn't be surprised if we influenced him in some way." In early 1965 Harrison gave his take on the subject of Dylan and The Beatles when he said: "I do know he likes our work and that knocks us out."

While there's no obvious Beatles influence in any of Dylan's songs, he was undoubtedly impressed with their ability and even admitted to being a fan. "It was obvious to me that they had staying power. In my head The Beatles were it," he said, and it's highly likely that they played a part in his decision to 'go electric'.

While it was McCartney who 'discovered' Dylan for The Beatles – he was alerted to *Freewheelin'* by a French DJ – it seems Lennon was the one most influenced by him.

"'You've Got To Hide Your Love Away' is my Dylan period," he said. "It's one of those you sing a bit sadly to yourself." Others reckoned that the song owed much to 'I Don't Believe In You' from *Another Side Of Bob Dylan*. But it wasn't all mutual back-slapping, as McCartney recalled when he took the band's Sgt *Pepper's Lonely Hearts Club Band* album round to Dylan's hotel room. "I remember playing some of *Sgt Pepper* and he said, 'Oh, I get it – you don't want to be cute any more'."

Whether it was the Beatles who directly influenced Dylan's decision to develop the fusion of folk and rock music and introduce electric guitars and amplification into his recording is something we can never be sure of. According to producer Wilson, who assembled the band on *Bringing It All Back Home*, only one man was

responsible for the move from folk to electric. "It came from me," he told Melody Maker in 1976. For his part, Dylan consistently told reporters that he didn't use an electric guitar "that much at all," before adding: "I just fool around with amplified sometimes."

However, in July 1965 Dylan took his new musical concept out of the studio and on to the road – and the result has gone down in the annals of rock music. At the Newport Folk Festival he was greeted with hostility when, after being introduced by folk singer Pete Yarrow from Peter, Paul and Mary, he walked on stage with a full amplified group, assembled from the Paul Butterfield Blues Band.

In front of the (apparently very loud) five-piece band, Dylan raced through three numbers – 'Maggie's Farm', 'Like A Rolling Stone' and 'Phantom Engineer' (later to appear as 'It Takes A Lot To Laugh, It Takes A Train To Cry') – in what was apparently a spontaneous, unplanned set. Greeted by boos, Dylan left the stage after three numbers, although it's possible they were the only songs the band had rehearsed.

Things were not helped by Dylan's rock-star appearance – black leather jacket, black slacks, a dress shirt and Cuban-heeled boots. The jeering and shouts of "Go back to the Sullivan Show!" seemingly hurt, surprised and upset Dylan, although he did return to the stage with an acoustic guitar, borrowed from Johnny Cash, to perform a solo spot.

Festival director Joe Boyd, later to produce Pink Floyd, The Incredible String Band and Fairport Convention, was not persuaded that the reaction was hostile, suggesting that "More!" and "Boo!" could sound similar when shouted by a huge crowd. "I think it was evenly divided between approbation and condemnation," he insisted.

While a backstage observer commented: "It seems to be one of the few times that Dylan was not in control," the man himself simply said: "It's all music, no more, no less." Four months later Dylan played Hartford, Connecticut, and after a 40-minute acoustic set reappeared with his band for the second half, to be immediately greeted with shouts of "Get rid of the band!" Undeterred, he worked his way through five numbers and, according to a newspaper review, "rocked it up" before leaving the stage, refusing all requests for a post-show interview.

Highway 61 Revisited

Before he embarked on his sixth album during the summer of 1965, Dylan travelled to London to play an eight-date tour filmed by D A Pennebaker as the fly-on-the-wall documentary *Don't Look Back*, released in 1967.

The filming also included what some consider the world's first music video, a sequence shot in an alley behind London's Savoy Hotel with Dylan holding up placards with the lyrics to 'Subterranean Homesick Blues'. During the visit Dylan explained that his still-acoustic show would last for "about an hour and a half," that he hadn't written any songs about Britain ("I didn't write: 'Mrs. Brown You Have A Lovely Cheese'") but that the plane trip had yielded a few ideas ("I made a few notes. I call it stabbing paper.")

Back in New York, Dylan settled back into Columbia's recording studios on Seventh Avenue, and this time he started out with Gregg and Griffin from the *Bringing It All Back Home* sessions, plus lead guitarist Michael Bloomfield and pianist Frank Owens. The sessions, with Wilson still in charge, began on June 15, when three songs were started, and ran on into the next day.

BELOW Captured on film by Donn Pennebaker (in top hat) for the *Don't Look Back* documentary.

RIGHT *Don't Look Back* promotional poster, 1967.

FAR RIGHT Dylan takes centre stage with The Byrds at Ciro's club in Los Angeles, California in 1965.

DYLAN
A FILM BY D. A. PENNEBAKER
DON'T LOOK BACK
ALAN PRICE   JOAN BAEZ

Just four days after his troubled appearance at the Newport Festival, Dylan returned to the studio with the same musicians, but this time without Wilson at the control desk. After working on five albums, he had been replaced by in-house Columbia producer Bob Johnston. He oversaw sessions between July 29 and August 4 when Al Kooper (guitar/organ), Harvey Goldstein (bass), Charlie McCoy (guitar) and Russ Savukus (bass) also arrived in the studio, becoming the first musicians to be credited on a Dylan album.

Altogether nine new Dylan songs were recorded with the new line-up with only one credited to former producer Wilson. This was opening track 'Like A Rolling Stone', a six-minute creation which had taken more than a dozen takes to perfect over the two days in June, with Kooper's first outing on organ making a memorable contribution to a song that topped *Rolling Stone*'s list of the 500 Greatest Songs Of All Time. Despite its length, it was released as a single and took Dylan into the top five in both the US and UK.

'Ballad Of A Thin Man' was started and completed on August 3 and it seems – despite a claim by Rolling Stone Brian Jones that he was an inspiration, and a suggestion that Joan Baez might even be 'Mr Joans' – that it could well be about *Village Voice* reporter Jeffrey Jones, who claimed he had interviewed and annoyed Dylan backstage at the Newport Festival.

Title track 'Highway 61 Revisited' is Dylan's paean to the main road

which ran from his birthplace, Duluth, Minnesota, to the Mississippi Delta, taking in the towns and cities that gave birth to music legends such as Muddy Waters and Elvis Presley; Bessie Smith was killed on the highway and Robert Johnson's famous pact to sell his soul to the devil was supposed to have taken place at its junction with Highway 49.

Dylan once said: "I always felt like I started on it [*Highway 61*], always had been on it and could go anywhere from it, even down into the deep Delta country," and he was insistent that this would be title of his new album, although he once told biographer Robert Shelton that it had been a fight: "Nobody understood it. I had to go up the fucking ladder until finally the word came down and said, 'Let him call it what he wants to call it'."

The nine-track album – three lasting more than five minutes – finishes with an extraordinary composition which runs out at over 11 minutes and was finally captured on the very last August 4 session. Dubbed by some as Dylan's alternative State of the Union Address, 'Desolation Row' was recorded as an 'electric take' on July 29 before the approved acoustic version – with visiting guitarist McCoy apparently joining Dylan – emerged from a combination of takes 6 and 7.

The album, with a cover photograph credited to Daniel Kramer plus unusual unaccredited shots of Dylan at the piano, ended up being Dylan's first top three album in America and a number four hit in the UK.

In the middle of recording *Highway 61 Revisited*, Dylan also spent time working on the song 'Positively 4th Street', which took its title from the street he had lived in Greenwich Village and was an obvious swipe at his former folk friends and fans who sneered at his Newport performance ("You gotta lot of nerve to say you're my friend.") Omitted from the album, it was released as a single and reached the top ten in both the US (number 7) and UK (number 8) in November 1965.

When Mick Hucknall decided to cover Dylan's 'Positively 4th Street' on his 2003 album *Home* he was attracted by one thing in particular. "I loved the lyrics. I like the acerbic, slightly bittersweet thing that he captures in so many of his lyrics. It also struck me as a song that I could do a new arrangement for, different to the one he'd done."

Highway 61 Revisited
Released August 1965. Tracks: Like A Rolling Stone / Tombstone Blues / It Takes A Lot to Laugh, It Takes A Train To Cry / From A Buick 6 / Ballad Of A Thin Man / Queen Jane Approximately / Highway 61 Revisited / Just Like Tom Thumb's Blues /.Desolation Row

LEFT Bob – with Grossman sitting in the background – listens carefully to a playback of his new album.

RIGHT Another pose for the official photographer in 1967.

OVERLEAF Shooting the 'Subterranean Homesick Blues' video in an alley behind London's Savoy Hotel with bearded beat poet Allen Ginsberg.

"I don't think
what comes out
of my music is
a call to arms ...
Songs are not
going to save
the world."

Bob Dylan, 1963

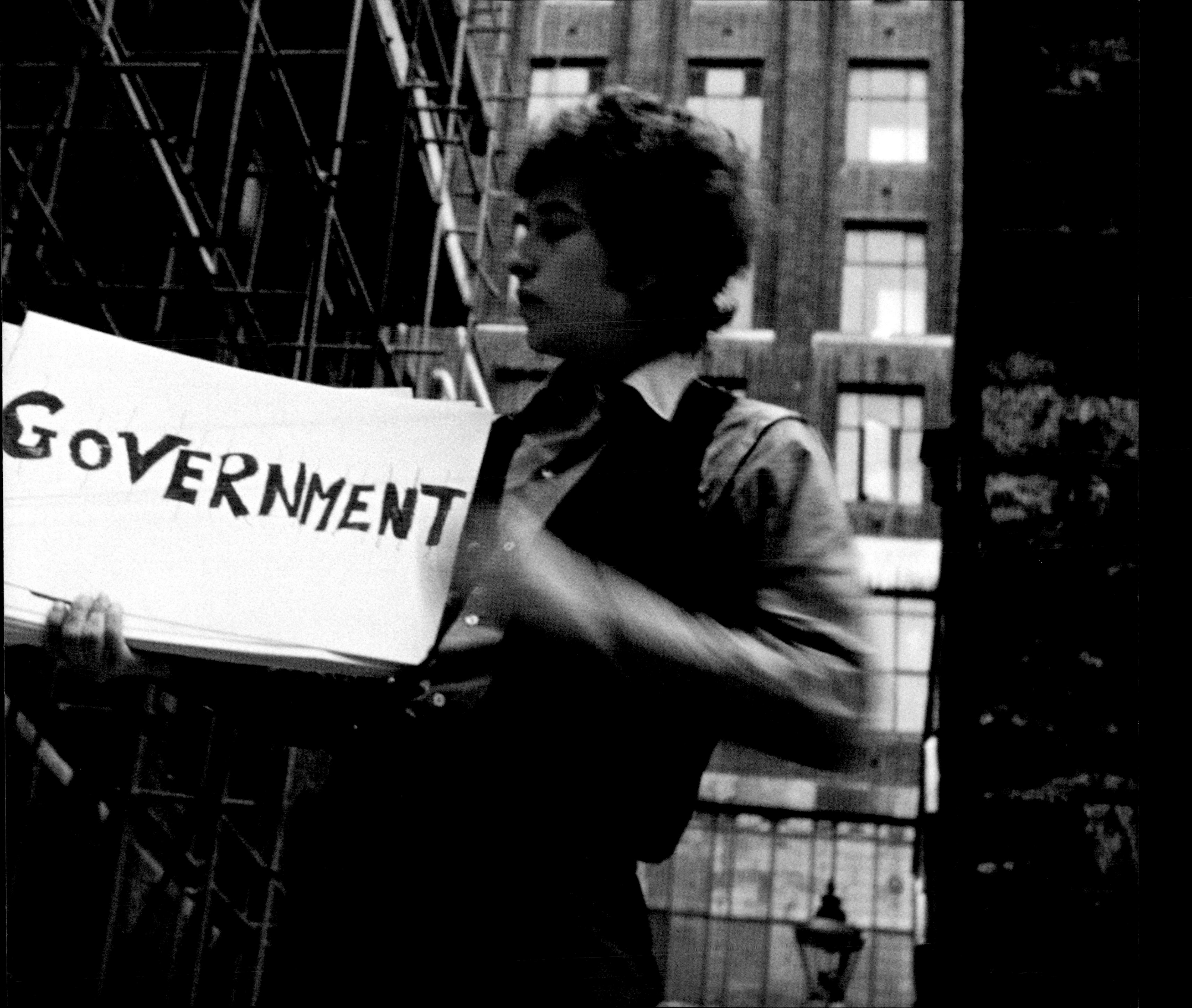
GOVERNMENT

Blonde On Blonde

After *Highway 61 Revisited* – and before marrying former model Sara Lowndes in November 1965 – Dylan focused his attention on hiring a new touring band. He was now committed to his new music although, interviewed in 1966, he dismissed the idea of musical genres: "As far as folk and folk-rock are concerned, it doesn't matter what kind of nasty name people invent for the music," he told *Playboy*. "I don't think that such a word as folk-rock has anything to do with it." Whatever it was called – and Dylan even suggested "arsenic music" – he needed to find the people to support him.

Blonde On Blonde

Released June 1966. Tracks: Rainy Day Women #12 & 35 / Pledging My Time / Visions Of Joanna / One Of Us Must Know (Sooner Or Later) / I Want You / Stuck Inside Of Mobile With The Memphis Blues Again / Leopard-Skin Pill-Box Hat / Just Like A Woman / Most Likely You Go Your Way And I'll Go Mine / Temporary Like Achilles / Absolutely Sweet Marie / 4th Time Around / Obviously Believers / Sad Eyed Lady Of The Lowlands

With Bloomfield and Kooper pulling out, Dylan was searching for musicians to join a mammoth nine-month tour covering the USA, Australia and Europe. He looked to Levon and The Hawks, who had gained recognition in Canada backing Ronnie Hawkins and also worked with John Hammond Jnr.

After a rehearsal in September 1965 and a debut in Austin, Texas, a week later, Dylan travelled to New York with Robbie Robertson (guitar), Rick Danko (bass), Richard Manuel (piano), Garth Hudson (organ) and drummer Levon Helm. They were to be the musicians on his seventh studio album, which he began recording in Columbia's studio on October 5. On November 30 they recorded a new single 'Can You Please Crawl Out Your Window' which was released in December but stalled at number 58 in America and peaked at number 17 in the UK. When Helm left, Gregg and Sandy Kanikoff were used for the remainder of the sessions in December and January.

Dylan and The Hawks in New York was a far from successful combination, and in five days of recording spread over four months only one album track was completed. A downhearted Dylan cancelled future sessions and told critic Robert Shelton: "I was really down. I mean, in ten recording sessions, man, we didn't get one song," presumably forgetting the one they had captured.

At the suggestion of new producer Bob Johnson, and despite manager Grossman's protests, Dylan moved to Columbia's Studio A in Nashville. He took Kooper and Robertson, while local musicians including Charlie McCoy (guitar, bass, harmonica), guitarist Wayne Moss, Joe South (guitar, bass) and drummer Kenny Buttrey

BELOW LEFT, BELOW and RIGHT Fresh from the studio, Dylan took the road with his new band The Hawks in 1966 and played dates in the US, Canada and Europe.

were recruited and even rehearsed, with a piano, in Dylan's hotel room. At the first Nashville session on February 14, 1966, two tracks were recorded, another at an all-nighter the next day and a fourth on the afternoon and evening of February 16.

After taking time out for shows with The Hawks in Canada and the US, Dylan returned to Nashville's famous Music Row in March and in just three days nine tracks were completed, bringing the final tally of album tracks to 14.

Blonde On Blonde was Dylan's first double album, with two songs, 'Visions Of Joanna' and 'Stuck Inside Of Mobile With The Memphis Blues Again', running over seven minutes and another over 11 minutes. Scheduled for release in May, it was delayed until summer and included 'One Of Us Must Know (Sooner Or Later)', the only survivor from the New York sessions.

'Rainy Day Women #12 & 35', with its compulsive refrain "Everybody must get stoned," was completed in one take on the last day in Nashville, and when Johnston suggested: "That sounds like the damn Salvation Army band." Dylan used McCoy on trumpet and local trombone player Wayne Butler to reinforce the feel. As a single, it was a US number two hit, became Dylan's second million-selling single and reached number seven in the UK.

'I Want You' is one of Dylan's most obvious pop songs, with a catchy melody and sing-along chorus, although he manages to mention undertakers, politicians and rock stars along the way; Brian Jones may well be the "dancing child with his Chinese suit". The third single off the album, it reached the Top 20 in both the US and the UK.

'Just Like A Woman' is thought to be about model and actress Edie Sedgwick, part of Andy Warhol's celebrated New York set. It combined what some saw as Dylan's cruellest lyrics with an uplifting melody and was his fourth single of 1966 but failed to make the US top 30 and wasn't released in Britain though Manfred Mann's version was a UK top 10 hit.

The final single from the album, 'Leopard-Skin Pill-Box Hat', was also supposedly inspired by Sedgwick, who some also believe inspired the title *Blonde On Blonde*. Released in April 1967, it just about crept into the US Hot 100.

Dylan's double album – in the days of vinyl – devoted its final side to his epic 'Sad Eyed Lady Of The Lowlands', started and finished overnight on February 15–16 and running for 11 minutes and 23 seconds – too long for most of the musicians, according to drummer Buttrey: "After about ten minutes of this thing we're cracking up at each other. I mean, we peaked five minutes ago."

The lady in the title was the new Mrs Dylan; while he began the song in New York before they were married, he didn't complete it until the day of recording in Nashville.

The *Blonde On Blonde* album made number nine in *Rolling Stone*'s 500 Greatest Albums list and hit the same chart spot in the US, going double platinum; it peaked at number three in the UK and earned Dylan his sixth Top Ten album.

"Judas!" The 1966 UK tour

With *Blonde On Blonde* successfully completed and a new band recruited
– even if they were more suited to touring than recording – Dylan and The
Hawks set off to visit Australia and Europe during the spring of 1966.

As at Newport and throughout the US the year before, the shows were split into two parts. The first half was solo Dylan with his trademark acoustic guitar and harmonica, while the second half involved Dylan and The Hawks playing high-energy, electric rock music.

The confrontation between die-hard folk purists and a broader, more rock-orientated audience was always likely to be volatile, but, once again, it seems that Dylan was not fully prepared for the fallout. It also appeared that he undertook the tour, at the end of a major trek across America, in less than perfect shape. He was worn out, and film-maker Pennebaker recalls that the singer was "taking a lot of amphetamine and who knows what else." Talking to *Rolling Stone* founder Jan Wenner three years after the tour, Dylan admitted: "I was on the road for almost five years. It wore me down."

Exhausted, Dylan arrived in Dublin for shows at the Adelphi Theatre on May 5 and 6 where, during his second-half performance, dozens of people walked out while others assailed him with shouts of "Traitor!" and "Leave it to The Rolling Stones!" Moving from Ireland to England, Dylan once again offered the media a less-than-satisfactory press conference which resulted in accusations that he was rude, arrogant and unco-operative.

New Musical Express writer Keith Altham admitted in his feature that he gave up after a couple of questions, including asking Dylan about singers Paul Simon and Bob Lind. "Never heard of them," was Dylan's reply. At the end of the event the journalist approached one of Dylan's aides – "I knew he was a Dylan man as he had dark glasses on" – and asked why such an obviously intelligent man bothered with such a farcical event. "Dylan just wanted us to come along and record a press reception so we could hear how ridiculous and infantile all reporters are," was the explanation.

However, *Melody Maker*'s Max Jones was luckier, and was treated to a brief one-on-one chat with Dylan in London. The music journalist asked Dylan if he was going to use an amplified guitar during his UK shows and was told: "I'm not sure if I will or not." Pressed further on the subject of protest songs, the American singer explained: "All my songs are protest songs. All I do is protest. You name it, I'll protest about it."

During shows in Bristol, Birmingham and Leicester there were more whistles and cat-calls during the second-half performances before the now legendary concert at Manchester's Free Trade Hall on May 17. Here a student, later identified as Keith Butler, was famously captured on tape shouting "Judas!" at Dylan. The singer replied: "I don't believe you," before adding: "You're a liar," and urging his band "to play fuckin' loud" as they launched into their closing number, 'Like A Rolling Stone'.

The European leg of Dylan's tour ended at London's Royal Albert Hall with shows on May 26 and 27 and, despite The Beatles and The Rolling Stones being in the hall, there were mass walkouts and heckling. While George Harrison suggested that the protesters were "idiots", the reviewers were less than impressed, with *Melody Maker*'s Ray Coleman describing the show as a shambles and *The Daily Telegraph* tagging Dylan as a performer "who does not care whether he communicates or not."

Speaking from the stage during the second half of his show on Friday, May 27, Dylan told the crowd: "I like my old songs. It's just that things change all the time." He went on to explain: "We've been playing this music since we were ten years old. Folk music was just an interruption and was very useful. If you don't like it (the new songs), that's fine."

After the show John Lennon and Paul McCartney made it back to Dylan's hotel suite where Lennon reportedly told the singer: "Best bloody show I've ever seen, Bob." The Rolling Stones also went along to the after-show event to meet Dylan, although Keith Richards, by his own admission, was "pretty frightened of him," while it seems Dylan was less than impressed by the songs The Stones wrote, as he told the band's lead guitarist: "I could write 'Satisfaction', but you couldn't write 'Mr Tambourine Man'."

Having announced on stage: "I'm not going to play any more concerts in England," Dylan left the UK and departed for a brief holiday in Spain before returning to New York to look at rushes of the documentary film *Don't Look Back*. On July 29, two months after his last London date, Dylan crashed his Triumph Bonneville 650 motorcycle near his home in Woodstock and reportedly suffered a broken neck vertebra. Few details have ever emerged about the crash or Dylan's injuries, but there's no doubt it came at a time when Dylan needed to ease up and take stock of his career and his life. "I was pretty wound up before the accident happened. I probably would have died if I'd kept on going the way I had been" was Dylan's own assessment of his situation in 1966.

BOB DYLAN

LIVE 1966
THE "ROYAL ALBERT HALL" CONCERT

FAR LEFT An exhausted Dylan hit the UK in May 1966.

LEFT A one-off poster for the infamous "Royal Albert Hall" concert, 1966. The poster become a pull-out gift that accompanied the *The Bootleg Series, Volume 4* album in 1998.

OVERLEAF Dylan heard the fans shout "traitor" and "Judas", but still played on in 1966.

John Wesley Harding

Whether he was recovering from the injuries sustained in his motorcycle accident or simply recuperating from a gruelling five years of touring and recording, Bob Dylan disappeared from the public gaze for more than 12 months during 1966 and 1967.

Rumours circulated that he was spending time in his Woodstock home working on a novel – he had signed a lucrative publishing deal some years earlier – in addition to pursuing his new interest in painting. He was also being a father to Sara's five-year-old daughter Maria and preparing for the birth of their son Jesse.

Either way, it was assumed that he wasn't actively pursuing his musical career, although it later transpired that The Hawks were busy in a studio they had set up in a rented house in Woodstock known as the Big Pink. Dylan was a regular visitor to the house, which was painted the colour of a strawberry milkshake, and during 1967 they recorded more than 100 songs together. "We were doing seven, eight … sometimes 15 songs a day," said the band's keyboard player Garth Hudson. These sessions inspired The Hawks to reappear as The Band and release their hugely successful debut album *Music From The Big Pink*.

Other recordings from the session turned up later on Dylan's 1975 album *The Basement Tapes*, while acts as diverse as Manfred Mann ('The Mighty Quinn'), Peter, Paul and Mary ('Too Much Of Nothing'), The Byrds ('You Ain't Goin' Nowhere') and Julie Driscoll, Brian Auger and The Trinity ('This Wheel's On Fire') all had hits with Dylan songs during 1968.

While fans had to make do with the 1967 release of a first *Greatest Hits* collection, which was a top ten hit in both America and Britain, Dylan signed a new and much improved recording deal with Columbia – his royalty was upped to ten per cent – in July 1967 and returned to the studio four months later.

Despite his sessions in Woodstock, Dylan decided to start afresh and once again travelled to Nashville to begin recording on October 17, 1967, with Bob Johnston back on the desk. He had a new set of songs but, according to The Band's Robbie Robertson, went to Tennessee "on a kind of whim" to record once again with drummer Kenny Buttrey and bassist Charlie McCoy, plus pedal steel guitarist Pete Drake.

Johnston recalled that Dylan first played him the songs he had in mind to record in his Nashville hotel room and "suggested that we should just use bass and guitar and drums on the record.

I said 'Fine', but also suggested we add a steel guitar." The whole album was completed in just three days of recording – October 17, November 6 and November 29 – and John Wesley Harding was released in the last week of December 1967, a turnaround of less than four weeks after the final sessions.

Although he returned to a more acoustic style, Dylan's stark and even austere presentation of his songs may have resulted from Woody Guthrie's death in September 1966, just a couple of weeks before recording began.

Talking to *Rolling Stone* magazine in 1969, Dylan explained the reasoning behind the album's title. "I called it that because I had that song 'John Wesley Harding'. It fits right in tempo. I was gonna

ABOVE Dylan offers his best side to the photographers.

LEFT The Hawks came from Canada and became bestsellers as The Band.

RIGHT Dylan and The Band remember Woody Guthrie at a New York memorial concert in 1968.

John Wesley Harding

Released 1967. Tracks: John Wesley Harding / As I Went Out One Morning / I Dreamed I Saw St Augustine / All Along The Watchtower / The Ballad Of Frankie Lee and Judas Priest / Drifters Escape / Dear Landlord / I Am A Lonesome Hobo / I Pity The Poor Immigrant / The Wicker Messenger Down Along The Cove / I'll Be Your Baby Tonight

write a ballad … a real long ballad. But in the middle of the second verse I got tired."

The album's title track was in fact completed on November 6, and tells of an American outlaw and gunfighter who was shot and killed in Texas in 1895.

'I'll Be Your Baby Tonight' is an up-tempo, country-flavoured, oddball love song which Dylan finished in the final three hours of the last day of recording.

The album's stand-out track 'All Along The Watchtower' also came from the second session in the first week of November and Dylan's album version differs from the live version he has offered up since 1970. The turning point was Jimi Hendrix's hard rock cover version which reached number 20 in the US and was a Top Five hit in the UK in 1968, two years before his death. Dylan explained, "I like Jimi Hendrix's record and ever since he died I've been doing it that way. When I sing I always feel it's a tribute to him in some kind of way."

At Dylan's insistence, *John Wesley Harding* was released with the minimum of promotion and publicity during the commercially 'dead' Christmas holiday period but it still managed to hit the number two spot in America and top the UK charts for a period of 13 weeks during 1968.

A week after the album's release Dylan returned to the stage for the first time since 1966 when he joined The Band at New York's Carnegie Hall for a concert in memory of Woody Guthrie.

Nashville Skyline

Following the enormous and even surprising success of *John Wesley Harding*, particularly in the light of Dylan's best efforts to under-promote the album, the singer spent much of 1969 concerned about his privacy ... or lack of it.

He had experienced intruders invading his property and suffered the displeasure of his neighbours – "To them it must've seemed I was something out of a carnival show," he commented – while the media continued to push him forward as a generation's spokesman. "I wasn't the toastmaster of a generation," was Dylan's reply to these assertions.

Nevertheless, he returned to Nashville in February 1969 to begin work on his ninth studio album, more than a year after his last recording sessions in 1967, and now he was intent on dipping into a new well of inspiration as he enveloped himself in the music America's southern states knew best – country.

He approached the sessions for *Nashville Skyline* with a collection of songs which, in his own words, were "easy to understand and there ain't too many words to remember." Once again Buttrey, McCoy and Drake were on hand to help out established producer Johnston and this time they were all joined by Bob Wilson (piano) and guitarists Norman Blake and Charlie Daniels.

Dylan and his half-dozen country players rattled through three tracks on February 13, four more on the following day and a further two on February 17. Explaining the rapid and easy-going studio work, Dylan recalled: "We just take a song, play it and everyone else just sort of fills in behind it. At the same time … there's someone in the control booth who's turning all the dials to where the proper sound is coming in." Throughout these sessions it was also apparent to everyone involved that Dylan had discovered a new, smooth, country-crooner singing voice which the man himself attributed to a break from smoking.

While Dylan was in Columbia's Nashville studio complex another major star was in the next studio, and pretty soon Dylan was working with Johnny Cash. During the final February 17 session they recorded three songs, but the next day they ran through a further 15 including 'That's Alright Mama', 'Mystery Train', 'I Walk The Line', 'Ring Of Fire', 'You Are My Sunshine' and 'Just A Closer Walk With Thee'. Ultimately all these duets were rejected, until it came to a song that had first appeared on *The Freewheelin' Bob Dylan* album six years earlier.

'Girl From The North Country' was one of the last songs Dylan and Cash recorded together in Nashville, and Dylan chose it as the opening track of his new album. Later, they also sang it on Cash's TV show, while Cash added his own personal and poetic liner notes to

the album: "This man can rhyme the track of time. The edge of pain, the what of sane." In 1969 Cash received a Grammy Award for Best Album Notes for his effort.

While 'Peggy Day' and 'One More Night' were dismissed as frivolous and the instrumental 'Nashville Skyline Rag' as unimportant, the whole of *Nashville Skyline* (which consisted of just ten tracks and lasted only 27 minutes) was condemned in some quarters as "routine" and "slight." Two singles were released from the album, 'I Threw It All Away' and 'Tonight I'll Be Staying Here With You', but both failed to get into the top 30 in either America or the UK.

However, there was one track which impressed critics and fans alike. 'Lay Lady Lay', completed on February 14, had been composed as a possible theme song for the film *Midnight Cowboy* but missed the deadline. Dylan later offered it to the Everly Brothers, only to have it rejected, and he then decided to record it himself. However, once it was

finished, he "begged and pleaded" with Columbia's bosses not to issue it as a single, explaining, "I was slightly embarrassed by it. I wasn't even sure I ever liked the song." In the end the label was proved right, as 'Lay Lady Lay' became Dylan's first top ten hit for three years – reaching number seven in the US and number five in the UK.

Bizarrely, *Nashville Skyline* was at one time set to be called John *Wesley Harding Volume II* or *Tonight I'll Be Staying Here With Peggy Day* and even *Peggy Day – Lay, Peggy Day*. "A lot of things were brought up. Some of the names just didn't seem to fit," Dylan confirmed. Eventually it peaked at number three in America and became his fourth UK number one album: but, perhaps more importantly, *Nashville Skyline* – despite its slightly strange country-bumpkin cover photograph of Dylan – introduced country music to a wider, more mainstream audience and opened the way for a host of new country rock artists.

Nashville Skyline
Released April 1969.
Tracks: Girl From The North Country / Nashville Skyline Rag / To Be Alone With You / Threw It All Away / Peggy Day / Lay Lady Lay / One More Night Tell Me That It Isn't True Country Pie / Tonight I'll Be Staying Here With You

LEFT A bespectacled Dylan takes a ride in the country.

RIGHT The quaint good ol' boy look Dylan adopted for the cover of *Nashville Skyline*.

Isle of Wight Festival 1969

Three years after he had suffered booing and heckling during concerts on his British tour, Dylan surprised almost everyone and returned to the United Kingdom to play a one-off concert in front of nearly 200,000 people on a small island located around three miles off England's south coast.

After his 1966 tour, when he introduced The Band and his 'new' electric sound to stunned audiences, and his motorcycle accident later the same year, *Melody Maker*'s respected folk writer Karl Dallas had predicted: "Bob Dylan is unlikely ever to appear in concert again," and when the singer turned down the opportunity to play in his own backyard at the inaugural Woodstock Festival in New York State in August 1969, it looked as though Dylan's career as a live performer might genuinely have come to an end.

Although the Woodstock site in Bethel was actually 60 miles away from his home in neighbouring Byrdcliffe, Dylan wasn't impressed with the idea of thousands of music fans rampaging around the area. After the four-day festival, which ran from August

15 to 18, he said, "It seemed to have something to do with me, this Woodstock nation and everything it represented. So we couldn't breathe. I couldn't get any space for me and my family."

While it was rumoured that the festival organizers had deliberately chosen Woodstock in an effort to persuade Dylan to come out of retirement, the plan backfired when he upped sticks and instead opted to perform at a festival which the year before had attracted 10,000 and been held on a farm to raise funds for a swimming pool.

Paid an impressive £50,000, Dylan flew first-class from America with his family and The Band for the second Isle of Wight festival, taking place in the village of Wootton over the August Bank

LEFT A smiling Dylan at the Isle of Wight festival.

RIGHT Relaxing by the sea during a British bank holiday.

Holiday weekend. This time, the thousands of fans paid either £2.10s (£2.50p) for a two-day pass or just £2 for a Sunday-only ticket and were entertained by the likes of Joe Cocker, Tom Paxton, and The Who, who closed Saturday's festivities.

During his brief stay on the island, famous for Parkhurst Prison and Queen Victoria's country residence of Osborne House, Dylan ensconced himself at Fernlands Farm and stayed pretty much out of sight, although he did appear at a brief press conference when he confirmed that it was "great to be here," and explained: "I don't want to protest any more" and outlined his set list with the words, "Everything we will do is on record."

While a number of the other acts included Dylan songs in their performances, the big Isle of Wight rumour was that George Harrison, The Rolling Stones and Blind Faith would join Dylan and his band on stage for an almighty jam session. In the end they all satisfied themselves by staying close to the stage and eventually watching Bob Dylan's very late, and very brief, return to the stage to top the bill on Sunday, August 30.

Two hours later than scheduled, he eventually went on stage at 11pm – explaining: "I was here at 5.30, ready to go on, but I was kept waiting until 11pm" – and surprised everyone by appearing with his hair neatly trimmed and dressed incongruously in a white suit.

During his disappointingly short set, Dylan ran through 17 songs, beginning with 'She Belongs To Me' and moving on to the hugely popular collection of 'Maggie's Farm', 'Mr. Tambourine Man', 'Lay Lady Lay', 'Like a Rolling Stone' and 'The Mighty Quinn' before closing with 'Rainy Day Women #12 & 35'. His explanation was simple. "I played long enough. I didn't want to go on much longer."

Melody Maker's reviewer described Dylan's performance as "a programme of mainly familiar Dylan compositions but in new vocal and instrumental settings. His voice sounded confident, well in tune and free of the old harshness." It was suggested that around 300 American journalists and broadcasters made their way to the Isle of Wight for Dylan's return to the stage – no

doubt disappointed by his non-appearance at their homeland Woodstock event.

Also in the crowd which assembled in a field on a farm was Apple Records executive Tony Bramwell, who travelled down with Eric Clapton, Jack Bruce and Ginger Baker from Cream especially to see Dylan. "We bussed into the backstage area just before Bob went on and watched his set from six feet in front of the stage," he said, before adding, "None of us was very impressed, so we got back on the bus and were back in London by one in the morning."

There's no doubt that Dylan's return to the stage disappointed those who had anticipated a three-hour show with a possible all-star finale, and the singer himself may been equally downhearted by the way things turned out. Before the festival he had spoken of his appearance as a comeback, but these plans were hastily shelved along with the idea of a live album recording of his long-awaited, over-hyped return. As the *New Musical Express* critic said, "The crowd obviously expected more but they didn't get it."

ABOVE After three years away, Dylan returned to the UK to play his late, late festival show behind a bank of microphones.

Self Portrait and New Morning

Ever enigmatic, Dylan moved on from his serious collection of country rock songs on *Nashville Skyline* to produce a double album which, although it failed to impress the critics, did continue his run of commercial successes.

He called *Self Portrait* "a bunch of tracks that we'd done all the time after I'd gone to Nashville. And then there was a lot of stuff that was just on the shelf." With Johnston again in charge, the sessions in Nashville and New York spanned nearly a year, from April 1969 to March 1970.

The result was Dylan's second double album, which featured around 50 musicians on two dozen tracks. Besides regulars Buttrey, McCoy, Drake and Kooper, there were all five of The Band plus string and horn sections, while the songs ranged from classics such as 'Blue Moon' and American backwoods song 'Copper Kettle' to live versions of 'Like A Rolling Stone', 'The Mighty Quinn' and 'She Belongs To Me', recorded live at the Isle of Wight.

Released in June 1970, it featured the country crooning voice Dylan had used earlier but this time strings, horns and a small choir were generously overdubbed. Some critics were savage – Greil Marcus' review in *Rolling Stone* opened with the line: "What is this shit?" – and Dylan seemed to acknowledge *Self Portrait* was a sub-standard offering, maybe even made as a joke and released "to get people off my back". However, it had at least one big fan – The

Who's Pete Townshend who said "It was a bit of a dip-in-and-see record, lots of different styles, and I was inspired by it. I thought, 'This guy is a great genius, no question about it'."

As to why it was a double album, Dylan bizarrely explained: "Well, it wouldn't have held up as a single album – then it really would've been bad. I mean if you're gonna put a lot of crap on it, you might as well load it up." Speaking in 1985, he went further and said: "I just figured I'd put all this stuff together and put it out: my own bootleg, so to speak."

Critics notwithstanding, it still reached number four in the US and was Dylan's third successive UK number one album. It also came with unique cover artwork. "I did this self-portrait for the cover," said Dylan. "I mean, there was no title for the album. I knew somebody who had some paints and a square canvas and I did the cover in about five minutes. And I said I'm gonna call the album *Self Portrait*."

Within five months of the release of his much-criticized double album, Dylan had issued a new LP, perhaps in an effort to reduce the damage done by *Self Portrait*.

Recorded in New York between June and August 1970, *New Morning* consisted of 12 new songs and marked the return of Dylan's familiar nasal singing voice. It was also apparent that many of the songs already existed when *Self Portrait* came out, although Dylan denied rushing the album out following criticism of his earlier effort. "It wasn't like that. It just happened coincidentally that one came out and then the other one did as soon as it did. We were working on *New Morning* when the *Self Portrait* album got put together."

In fact, during sessions for the earlier album Dylan began recording songs that would eventually appear on *New Morning*, although they were re-worked before inclusion. Among the musicians who joined him for the *New Morning* sessions on May 1, 1970, were George Harrison, Charlie Daniels and drummer Russ Kunkel.

In spring 1970 Dylan agreed to provide songs for poet Archibald MacLeish's play, *Scratch*, and duly created 'New Morning', 'Times Passes Slowly' and 'Father Of The Night'. However, following a

ABOVE On stage in Los Angeles at the 1970 Woody Guthrie memorial show.

LEFT Bob Dylan & Johnny Cash duet on TV.

RIGHT George Harrison and Dylan performing in New York during the 1971 Concert for Bangla Desh at Madison Square Garden.

Self Portrait

Released 1970. Tracks: All The Tired Horses / Alberta #1 I Forgot More Than You'll Ever Know / Days Of 49 / Early Morning Rain / In Search Of Little Sadie / Let It Be Me / Little Sadie / Woogieboogie / Belle Isle / Living The Blues / Like A Rolling Stone / Copper Kettle / I Gotta Travel On / Blue Moon The Boxer / Quinn The Eskimo / Take Me As I Am / Take A Message To Mary / It Hurts Me Too / Minstrel Boy / She Belongs To Me / Wigwam / Alberta #2

dispute with the producer he withdrew his songs from the play but included them on his new album.

From June 1 to 5, ensconced in Columbia's Studio E, Dylan completed most of the work for his album. Sessions on July 13 and 23 yielded some rejected efforts but on August 12 Dylan finally completed the last tracks for *New Morning* in the company of Kooper. He had taken over as producer from Johnston who, it seems, departed some time in July, leaving Kooper to deal with Dylan's demands. "When I finished the album I never wanted to speak to him again", commented Kooper. "He changed his mind every three

seconds so I ended up doing the work of three albums."

The song 'Went To See The Gypsy' chronicles a supposed get-together between Dylan and Elvis Presley, though there's no hard evidence they ever met. Dylan did, however, go to see him at Madison Square Garden in 1972, two years after recording this song.

'If Not For You' is one of Dylan's more uplifting love songs and again features Kooper's distinctive organ-playing. A duet with George Harrison was recorded but not included on the album (although Harrison featured it on his *All Things Must Pass* album) and it was left to Olivia Newton-John to release it as her debut chart single in 1971.

New Morning took Dylan's tally of UK number one albums to six – four in succession – and while it peaked at number seven in the US, it did become his eighth top ten album in seven years.

New Morning

Released 1970. Tracks: If Not For You / Day Of The Locusts
Time Passes Slowly / Went To See The Gypsy / Winterlude /
If Dogs Run Free / New Morning / Sign On The Window / One
More Weekend / The Man In Me / Three Angels / Father of the
Night

Dylan at the Movies

Bob Dylan's first involvement with the film *Pat Garrett And Billy The Kid* came in late 1972 when he was sent the screenplay by writer Rudy Wurlitzer with an invitation to write a couple of songs for the soundtrack.

Immediately attracted by the idea of actually having a role in the film, Dylan travelled to Mexico to meet director Sam Peckinpah, a man apparently completely unaware of Dylan's standing as a rock musician. However, when Dylan played him the song 'Billy', he was moved to offer him a part as 'Alias', a member of the outlaw gang.

Working alongside James Coburn as Sheriff Pat Garrett and Kris Kristofferson as Billy the Kid, Dylan worked in Durango, Mexico, from late 1972 until early 1973 – with a break for Christmas – but found his role being slowly reduced as Peckinpah grew more unstable and irascible. "There I was, trapped deep in the heart of Mexico. With some madman," was the singer's assessment of his movie debut. While his role drew a favourable response from Kristofferson – "You see him on the screen and all eyes are on him. There's something about him that's magnetic" – the critics were less impressed, one describing his acting as "an assortment of tics, smirks, winks, shrugs and smiles."

The first session for the soundtrack album took place in the CBS Discos studios in Mexico City on January 20, when 'Billy 7' was successfully recorded, before Dylan moved to work in the Burbank studios in Los Angeles in February, where he completed the remaining nine tracks including the stand-out song chosen as his new single. While the album hit the top 20 in America and the top 30 in the UK, 'Knockin' On Heaven's Door' became his best-selling single for four years and has been successfully covered by both Eric Clapton and Guns N' Roses.

Having been passed over for the role of Woody Guthrie in the film *Bound For Glory* (the part went to David Carradine), Dylan opted to make his own movie in 1975. His *Rolling Thunder* touring revue provided the setting for *Renaldo And Clara*, which Dylan directed, co-wrote with Sam Shepherd and starred in alongside his wife Sara, ex-girlfriend Joan Baez, singer Ronnie Hawkins (who appears as Bob Dylan) and poet Allen Ginsberg, plus Harry Dean

ABOVE Dylan's white-faced image from *Renaldo and Clara*. **RIGHT** As 'Alias' in *Pat Garret and Billy The Kid*.

Stanton, who appeared in *Pat Garrett And Billy The Kid*.

As there was no discernible plot, the film – which ran for nearly four hours – ended up as part-documentary and part-improvization with narrative-free passages, scenes of concert performances and footage of singers Phil Ochs and David Blue, plus boxer Rubin Carter. After its initial showing in 1978, when it was savaged by the critics, Dylan created a shorter two-hour version but eventually he withdrew the film from circulation.

Almost a decade after *Renaldo And Clara*, Dylan returned to the big screen to play rock legend-turned-chicken farmer Billy Parker in *Hearts Of Fire*, directed by Richard Marquand (famous for *Return of the Jedi* and *Jagged Edge*) and starring Fiona Flanagan as Dylan's love interest and Englishman Rupert Everett as a rival, youthful rock star. Even though he contributed two songs – 'Had A Dream About You Baby' and 'Night After Night' – plus cover versions of 'The Usual' and 'Couple More Years', the majority of the music was created by composer John Barry. Filmed in Canada, England and Wales, with concert footage shot in Bristol's Colston Hall and in Camden, London, *Hearts Of Fire* was released in 1987 to such poor reviews that it was withdrawn from the UK cinema circuit after just two weeks and never released to theatres in America.

Having played a rock star in one film, Dylan did it again in 2003, appearing as Jack Fate in the 'comedy-drama' *Masked And Anonymous*, directed by Larry Charles, the successful writer of TV's *Seinfeld* and *Mad About You*.

With a stellar cast including John Goodman, Jeff Bridges, Penelope Cruz, Val Kilmer, Mickey Rourke and Jessica Lange – plus a script co-written by Dylan, under the alias Sergei Petrov – the film is set around 'Fate' being released from prison to play a one-man benefit concert to help the victims of a rapidly decaying American society.

The music was supplied by Dylan and his regular touring band of Charlie Sexton, Larry Campbell, Tony Garnier and George Receli, who appear as Fate's backing band Simple Twist Of Fate; between them they perform versions of 'Blowin' In the Wind', 'Dirt Road Blues', 'Not Dark Yet' and 'A Hard Rain's Gonna Fall'.

Shot in just three weeks for around $7 million – some of the cast worked for the union rate in order to appear with Dylan – *Masked And Anonymous* was launched at the 2003 Sundance Film Festival, where it was reviewed as "a vanity production beyond reason." As a result of the poor reaction, the film was denied a theatrical release in the UK.

LEFT Playing the rock star Billy Parker in *Heart of Fire*.

ABOVE In costume and on the set for *Masked And Anonymous*.

Planet Waves and Before The Flood

The end of the 1960s also saw Bob Dylan bring the curtain down on two long relationships in his professional career as a musician.

When his contract with manager Albert Grossman came up for renewal around the time of the Woodstock Festival, Dylan decided it was time he took charge of his own affairs with the help of advisers. This meant that it was very much his own decision to leave Columbia Records when his contract with the label he joined in 1962 came up for renewal in 1973.

The prospect of Bob Dylan being a free agent brought out the music industry's big guns, as almost every major label went after the million-selling singer-songwriter. At the front of the queue was David Geffen, who had founded Asylum Records in 1972 after a period co-managing Joni Mitchell, Jackson Browne and Crosby, Stills and Nash.

So determined was Geffen to sign Dylan that he courted his friend Robbie Robertson, from The Band, and even held meetings with Dylan on the beach near the singer's home in Malibu, California. Eventually Geffen got his man to sign to his Asylum label, his plan being not only to release Dylan's records but also to get him back on the road with The Band.

The first Asylum album came about following rehearsals with The Band in Malibu, which prompted Dylan to head for New York in October 1973 to compose new material. By the time he returned and went into the Village Recorders studio in Los Angeles in November, he had nine new songs. Between November 2 and 14, under the direction of producer/engineer Rob Fraboni, Dylan and The Band then completed the new album, which had the working title *Ceremonies Of The Horsemen*.

ABOVE Dylan returned to the stage to tour America in 1974.

RIGHT A poster for his 1974 tour with The Band.

OPPOSITE LEFT Ten shows were recorded for a live album.

OPPOSITE RIGHT The Band's Rick Danko and Robbie Robertson with Dylan.

Planet Waves

Released 1974. Tracks: On A Night Like This / Going Going Gone / Tough Mama / Hazel / Something There Is About You Forever Young / Dirge / You Angel You / Never Say Goodbye / Wedding Song

The first, and only, studio album Dylan ever recorded with The Band was particularly memorable for Fraboni who said: "It was striking to do something that powerful that quickly." Closing track 'Wedding Song' is an example of how rapidly things happened; Dylan wrote it lying on the floor of the control room and then recorded it in one take on November 9. 'Forever Young', on the other hand, was started – without drummer Levon Helm, who was still making his way to California – on November 4,

Before The Flood

Released 1975. Tracks: Most Likely You Go Your Way (And I'll Go Mine) / Lay Lady Lay / Rainy Day Women #12 & 35 Knockin' On Heaven's Door / It Ain't Me Babe / Ballad Of A Thin Man / Up On Cripple Creek / I Shall Be Released / Endless Highway / The Night They Drove Old Dixie Down / Stage Fright / Don't Think Twice It's Alright / Just Like A Woman It's Alright Ma / The Shape I'm In / When You Awake / The Weight / All Along The Watchtower / Highway 61 Revisited Like A Rolling Stone / Blowin' In The Wind.

attempted again on November 5 and then on November 8, 9 and 14. Dylan told Fraboni: "I been carrying this song around in my head for five years and I never wrote it down and now I come to record it, I just can't decide how to do it." In the end two different master takes from two separate sessions were included on the album, now retitled *Planet Waves*.

Once again the album's artwork was a painting by Dylan and it contains the words 'Cast-Iron Songs And Torch Ballads' plus a Campaign for Nuclear Disarmament (CND) symbol. *Planet Waves* came out on the Island label in the UK, where it reached number seven, while his only studio album for Asylum would finally see Bob Dylan reach number one in the US … and stay there for five weeks.

Back on the road for the first time since his 1966 tour, Bob Dylan took The Band on a 39-date tour of America in January 1974 and the public's response was overwhelming – with more than five million applications for a total of 660,000 tickets. But according to *Melody Maker*'s man in New York, who saw a Thursday afternoon show in Madison Square Garden, the only

words Dylan spoke during the show were "Back in ten minutes" when it came to the half-time interval.

Ahead of the tour, Dylan and his label Asylum decided on a spread of ten separate live recordings in venues around the country – three at Madison Square Garden in New York, two at Seattle's Center Coliseum, two more in Oakland's Alameda County Coliseum and three at the Los Angeles Forum.

In the event, the double album *Before The Flood* consisted of 20 tracks recorded in Los Angeles, plus one song – 'Knockin' On Heaven's Door' – from New York, and also included eight songs by The Band, including 'Up On Cripple Creek', 'Stage Fright' and 'The Weight'. While some classic Dylan songs were missing, there were impressive versions of 'All Along The Watchtower', 'Like A Rolling Stone' and 'Lay Lady Lay' plus a brief acoustic set featuring 'Don't Think Twice It's Alright', 'Just Like A Woman' and 'It's Alright Ma'. Some have suggested the album's title refers to the idea of releasing the official live album before the inevitable flood of bootlegs.

Before The Flood was a number three hit in America and reached number eight in the UK.

Blood On The Tracks and The Rolling Thunder Revue

Dylan's return to live work in 1974 profoundly affected the life of domestic bliss he had seemingly been living since his marriage to Sara in 1965. He was thrown back into life on the road and soon discovered it could be enjoyable and inspirational. By the time the tour was over, he was involved with record executive Ellen Bernstein and separated from his wife.

Back in New York, Dylan revisited his old Greenwich Village haunts and even began to take painting classes before returning to his Minnesota farm to begin the songs for his next album.

Having re-signed with Columbia, where Bernstein worked, Dylan moved into the old Columbia studios in New York, now renamed A&R Studios, with Phil Ramone acting as engineer to Dylan the producer. "Never turning off the tape machine was part of the way you recorded Dylan," explained Ramone.

Banjo player Eric Weissberg and his band Deliverance were hired, and quickly fired, to be replaced by bass player Tony Brown, organist Paul Griffin and steel guitarist Buddy Cage for sessions that ran from September 16 to 19. During those three days Dylan recorded, mixed and even cut a test pressing of the new album which Columbia was all set to release, until Dylan returned to the Sound 80 Studios in Minnesota in December.

Here, in three days immediately following Christmas, Dylan re-recorded six songs with a selection of local players and rewrote some lyrics during time with his children and brother. *Blood On The Tracks* was released in January 1975 with ten tracks and a strange, mottled, profile shot of Dylan on the cover.

Opening track 'Tangled Up In Blue' is a long, narrative work which some have called his finest song. While he once said it took him "ten years to love and two years to write," it was in fact written during time spent on his Minnesota farm without his wife in 1974. On the other hand, 'You're Gonna Make Me Lonesome When You Go' is about the other woman in his life, Ellen Bernstein, and seemingly continues the album's themes of loneliness, sorrow and anger.

'Idiot Wind' – at just under eight minutes – was finished in New York and then dramatically altered when Dylan got to Minnesota,

where he made it more personal and arguably even more bitter. While Dylan's son Jakob once claimed the songs on *Blood On The Tracks* "are my parents talking," Dylan himself remarked to his old friend Mary Travers (from Peter, Paul and Mary): "A lot of people told me they enjoyed that album. It's hard for me to relate to that … people enjoying that type of pain."

Painful and personal as it may have been, *Blood On The Tracks*, after receiving less than impressive initial reviews, has since been acknowledged as one of Dylan's greatest works, *Daily Telegraph* writer Neil McCormick suggested it's "the most intricate, eloquent and savagely remorseless examination of the downside of love ever committed to record."

The album, described by Ramone as "a major turnaround" in Dylan's life, became his second successive US number one and peaked at number four in the UK, though single 'Tangled Up In Blue' stalled at number 31 in the US.

ABOVE The Rolling Thunder Revue kicked off in October 1975.

LEFT On stage at a San Francisco benefit in March 1975.

RIGHT Dylan (second from right) on stage with (L to R) Richie Havens, Joan Baez and Ramblin' Jack Elliott.

Blood On The Tracks
Released 1975. Tracks: Tangled Up in Blue / Simple Twist Of Fate / You're A Big Girl Now / Idiot Wind / You're Gonna Make Me Lonesome When You Go / Meet Me In the Morning / Lily Rosemary and Jack Of Hearts / If You See Her Say Hello / Shelter From The Storm / Buckets Of Rain

Having toured America in 1974, Dylan embarked on a new concept in touring in late 1975 with the Rolling Thunder Revue, featuring the likes of Baez, Roger McGuinn, Joni Mitchell, Allen Ginsberg, David Blue and Ramblin' Jack Elliott as walk-on guests in a giant travelling circus.

Also recruited for the two legs of the Rolling Thunder Revue – named, it seems, either after a Native American shaman, America's Vietnam bombing campaign or Dylan's own suggestion that he heard "Boom, boom, boom, boom rolling from west to east" – was English guitarist Mick Ronson. Previously one of David Bowie's Spiders From Mars, he recalled Dylan phoned him two days before rehearsals began and asked: "Would I be there?" After touring the US between October and December 1974 and again in April and May 1976, Ronson said: "The whole thing was an adventure, a treasure hunt." Part of Dylan's thinking, he said, was "to embark upon the New England dates to celebrate in some way America's bicentennial year".

He also confirmed: "He doesn't talk much at all. He's just around and you know he's there. He doesn't have to say anything."

The Rolling Thunder Revue closed its first run with a major show at Madison Square Garden on December 8, a benefit for boxer Rubin 'Hurricane' Carter, whom many believed to have been wrongfully convicted of murder. The show, Night Of The Hurricane, was hosted by Muhammed Ali and also featured Roberta Flack.

"All my songs are protest songs. All I do is protest. You name it, I'll protest about it."

Bob Dylan, 1966

LEFT Performing the Rolling Thunder Revue, Harvard Square Theater, Massachusetts, 1975
RIGHT Rolling Thunder Revue poster, 1975–76.

ROLLING THUNDER REVUE

STARRING
BOB DYLAN
JOAN BAEZ · JACK ELLIOTT
BOB NEUWIRTH

HARVARD SQUARE THEATER
Cambridge, Massachusetts
Thursday, November 20th   8:00 p.m.
Reserved Seating $8.50   Limit 2 tickets per person
On sale at Harvard Square Theater

ZEBRA CONCERTS, INC.

Desire, Hard Rain and Street Legal

Before embarking on his Rolling Thunder Revue, Dylan began work on a new album, this time with a co-writer. Jacques Levy had collaborated with Roger McGuinn to create The Byrds' hit 'Chestnut Mare', and a meeting with Dylan in Greenwich Village sparked a friendship which resulted in Dylan asking him to write some material for him.

ABOVE Dylan on stage during his 1978 *Street Legal* world tour.

RIGHT An original 8-track cassette for 1978's *Street Legal*.

Hard Rain
Released 1976. Tracks: Maggie's Farm / One Too Many Mornings / Stuck Inside Of Mobile / Oh Sister / Lay Lady Lay Shelter From The Storm / You're A Big Girl Now / I Threw It All Away / Idiot Wind.

On July 14, 1975, in Columbia's New York studio, Dylan finally began work on the first songs he and Levy had created, 'Joey', an epic ballad about the gangster Joey Gallo, and 'Rita Mae', a short song about Rita Mae Brown, the lesbian writer. For the next three weeks the new writing partnership shifted to the Hamptons in upstate New York, where they finished the songs for the album that would be called *Desire*.

Back in the studio on July 30, with the likes of Emmylou Harris, violinist Scarlett Rivera, bass player Rob Stoner and drummer Howie Wyeth, Dylan completed seven songs for the new album, and on the following day he finished both 'Isis' and 'Sara', two songs about his wife, who was with him at the session.

Desire, Dylan's third successive chart-topping album in America and a number three hit in the UK, also featured the song Dylan and Levy had written about the boxer Rubin 'Hurricane' Carter, who had been arrested for murder in 1966. Dylan held concerts in support of Carter as part of the Rolling Thunder Revue while 'Hurricane' an 11-minute song and a top 50 hit in both the US and the UK, helped the fighter get his conviction overturned in 1985.

Recorded live at Hughes Stadium in Fort Collins, Colorado, on May 23, during the second section of the Rolling Thunder Revue, the release of album *Hard Rain* coincided with the broadcast in September 1976 of an NBC TV special of the same name, sponsored by Craig Powerplay Car Stereo and Audio Components.

After an earlier recording from a Florida show had been rejected, Dylan paid for the Colorado show to be taped on the eve of his 35th birthday. With wife Sara in the audience, the show was a rip-roaring performance which impressed bass player Stoner: "It's like a punk record. It's got such energy and anger."

Although it was entitled *Hard Rain*, Dylan's 'A Hard Rain's Gonna Fall' was missing from the album but was the opening track of the TV show, while he threw in a new arrangement of 'Maggie's Farm' and performed 'Lay Lady Lay' with some raunchy new lyrics. *Hard Rain* peaked at number 17 in America but followed *Desire* to the number three spot in the UK.

After releasing the *Desire* and *Hard Rain* albums Dylan became preoccupied with domestic matters, as Sara successfully filed for divorce in the summer of 1977. He distracted himself with preparations for a world tour and with a new album, which he began after the Japanese and Australian dates were over.

With a group consisting in the main of musicians from his touring band – including Rob Stoner, David Mansfield, Jesse Ed Davis, Ian Wallace, Billy Cross, Bobbye Hall, Steve Douglas and Jerry Scheff – Dylan, using his own Rundown Studio in Los Angeles, cut all nine tracks on the *Street Legal* album in just five days during April 1978. "We couldn't find the right producer so we just brought in the remote truck … and went for a live sound," he said later.

Street Legal got to number 11 in the US but went to number 2 – and was certified platinum – in the UK, where sales were boosted by his arrival in the UK in June 1978 (for the first since 1966) to play six shows at Earls Court plus the Blackbushe Aerodrome festival in July, for which he was reportedly paid a grand total of £650,000.

Desire
Released 1976. Tracks: Hurricane / Isis / Mozambique / One More Cup Of Coffee / Oh Sister / Joey / Romance In Durango Black Diamond Bay / Sara.

Working with Dylan in the UK was CBS press officer Elly Smith, who recalled delivering some music to his London hotel room. "I wondered if he was aware of the punk thing that was going on so I got some of my records together and put them in his room. I remember writing a note and began worrying whether I should say, 'Dear Mr Dylan', 'Dear Bob' or just 'Bob'."

After Dylan had commented on Smith's leather jacket and asked if she would take him shopping, she received a phone call in her hotel room. "This voice said 'Is that Elly? This is Bob'. He said he'd been listening to the records and wanted me to go to his room and talk about them. He was really interested in the music. I don't think he'd been exposed to very much punk before."

With Dylan making it clear to his record company that he wasn't going to do any interviews or promote *Street Legal* in any way other than by playing his concerts – "Everything on the tour was very disciplined, he was always on time and there were never any tantrums," recalls Smith – it left time for what he liked doing most.

"He wanted to go to gigs so I took him to Dingwalls to see Elvis Costello," says Smith. "I had a pass for me and a guest, but the guy on the door said that there was no room for any guests. Then he looked at my guest, saw it was Bob Dylan and said, 'OK he can come in'." However, a plan to go to Dalston in East London to hear some reggae in a club recommended by The Clash's Joe Strummer was abandoned when the management decided it was too dangerous.

Smith's one lasting disappointment is that while she got Dylan to autograph a bunch of his albums for a competition, she never got a copy signed for herself. "I would really have loved him to have done one for me but I couldn't ask him because I didn't want to look like a fan. I was very aware of being professional," says Smith, an American who went on to work at Virgin and Sire.

LEFT In-store advertising poster for *Hard Rain*, 1976.

BELOW Ticket stub from Bob Dylan and The Band concert at Nassau County Auditorium, NY, January 28, 1974.

BELOW RIGHT Ticket stub from 1978's Rolling Thunder Revue concert at Hartford, US, on November 22, 1975.

Street Legal

Released June 1978. Tracks: Changing Of the Guards / New Pony / No Time To Think / Baby Stop Crying / Is Your Love In Vain? / Senor (Tales Of Yankee Power) / True Love Tends To Forget / We Better Talk This Over / Where Are You Tonight?

GUEST

BOB DYLAN

Miami, Fla.
Dec. 16, 1978

ABOVE Guest pass for a Miami, Florida, show 1978.

LEFT The man behind the shades posing for a 1978 portrait.

RIGHT Relaxing on the tour bus as they travel through London, 1978.

The Gospel Years

At the end of Dylan's 1978 world tour, the man returned to America to play a further 64 shows spread over 92 days, beginning in Augusta, Georgia, on September 15. Originally dubbed "the alimony tour", it was later called "the Vegas tour" as Dylan was criticized for allegedly running through his greatest hits in a cabaret-style set.

In response to suggestions that he'd gone cabaret or even disco, Dylan said: "I don't know how they come up with these theories. We never heard them when we played Australia, Japan or Europe." Much of the bad press had been prompted by his baffling film *Renaldo and Clara* and the less-than-perfect *Street Legal* album.

One man who crossed Dylan's path during the US tour was Keith Emerson, keyboard player with ELP, who played the same venue one day after Dylan. "The promoter invited me to go to a hotel suite where there was to be a party," recalls Emerson. "I sat around for about 45 minutes after Bob's performance and there was no sign of the great man until he came in, walked right past everyone and went into his bedroom."

Persuaded by the promoter not to leave, Emerson finally got to meet Dylan and recalls how the conversation went. "Bob said, 'Where you from?' and I said, 'England; where you from?' He sort of nodded in a northerly direction. We both realized it wasn't going to be a very scintillating conversation. Bob shrugged his shoulders and I went to my room wondering what all that had been about."

In the middle of his American dates, Dylan played a gig in San Diego in November while feeling unwell. "I think the crowd could see that. And they threw a silver cross on the stage," said Dylan, who rarely collected things thrown by the audience. "I picked up the cross and I put it my pocket and I brought it to the next town, which was in Arizona ... I was feeling even worse. I said 'I need something tonight that I didn't have before' and I looked in my pocket and I had this cross."

Dylan would later explain that in his hotel room in Tucson, Arizona, he had a vision of Christ. "Jesus did appear to me as King of Kings and Lord of Lords," he said. "There was a presence in the room that couldn't have been anybody but Jesus." Slowly, with the same silver cross around his neck, Dylan began to change the lyrics of his songs to include Bible references, and as the tour drew to its close he began writing songs that would reflect his new-found conversion to Christianity.

Dylan had also begun to attend courses at the Vineyard Fellowship, a Christian organization based in California, before he went into the famous Muscle Shoals studio in Miami to start recording at

the end of April 1979, He recruited Dire Straits guitarist Mark Knopfler and legendary producer Jerry Wexler to work on the album alongside drummer Pick Withers, keyboardist (and co-producer) Barry Beckett, bassist Tim Drummond, singers Carolyn Dennis and Helena Springs plus the famous Muscle Shoals Horns.

Between April 30 and May 11 they worked their way through nine songs, finishing up with 'When He Returns', which closed the album, called *Slow Train Coming*, and featured Dylan's hastily rehearsed lead vocal over Beckett's piano track.

'Gotta Save Somebody' displayed Dylan's new enthusiasm for rock gospel singing and the top 30 US single earned him the 1980 Grammy Award for Best Rock Vocal Performance.

The track 'Slow Train' was a song which Dylan debuted at a sound check for a show near the end of his 1978 US tour and came close to alienating many of his fans, who suspected their man of something akin to American jingoism.

Slow Train Coming took Dylan back into the US top three, and in the UK it followed *Street Legal* to the number two spot.

Dylan was back at Muscle Shoals just nine months after making *Slow Train Coming*, in February 1980, and once again Wexler and Beckett were in charge of production for the sessions, which featured Beckett, Dennis and Drummond alongside drummer Jim Keltner and Spooner Oldham on keyboards.

The nine songs on *Saved* continued Dylan's Christian theme following his religious conversion, with one review saying the album was an "open declaration of Dylan's deepening faith." While Dylan composed seven of the tracks, he co-wrote the title track with Drummond and opened the album with a 1950s country classic. 'A Satisfied Mind' was written by Red Hayes and Jack Rhodes, and covered by both Ella Fitzgerald and The Byrds, but the high spot was Porter Wagoner's 1955 version, which topped the US country chart.

Dylan's 20th studio album, *Saved* was not a commercial success in America, where it peaked at number 24 (his first album since *Another Side Of Bob Dylan* in 1964 not to reach the top 20) but it went to number three in the UK and became his tenth successive top 10 album.

LEFT AND OPPOSITE By 1979 Dylan's shows had begun to reflect his move to Christianity.

OVERLEAF Performing with his 'heavenly choir' during the tours for *Slow Train Coming* and *Saved*.

Saved

Released 1980. Tracks: A Satisfied Mind / Saved / Covenant Woman / What Can I Do For You? / Solid Rock / Pressing On In the Garden / Saving Grace / Are You Ready?

The Wilderness Years

In 1981 Dylan completed his trilogy of religious albums with the release of *Shot of Love*, which also showed the first signs of his return to secular songs. It continued his run of UK top 10 albums, peaking at number 6, but missed the top 30 in America despite Dylan's assertion that it was the "most explosive" album he'd made.

While many critics didn't agree, Dylan still set off on his *Shot of Love* tour of America, proving that he could still fill auditoriums across the country. By the time he came to record *Infidels* in 1983 Dylan's religious fervour was on the wane, although he chose to release an album with just eight tracks while discarding a further eight including 'Blind Willie McTell', his tribute to the blues musician.

Co-produced with Mark Knopfler and featuring former Rolling Stones guitarist Mick Taylor, *Infidels* boasted the single 'Jokerman' which, despite Dylan being persuaded to make his first video for MTV, failed to chart in either the UK or the US. The album, however, was a bestseller, reaching number 20 in America and becoming another UK top 10 hit – his 23rd.

Dylan was back on the road in 1984 and three shows – recorded in Dublin, London and Newcastle – formed his *Real Live* album release. Critics called the choice of songs "hopeless," described the performances as "inadequate" and panned the productions as "inexcusable," even though he was backed by Taylor, Faces' keyboardist Ian McLagan and guitarist Carlos Santana. The ten-track collection missed the UK top 50 and also failed to enter the US Top 100.

Fresh from taking part in the USA For Africa recording of 'We Are The World' in January 1985, Dylan returned to the studios to embark on *Empire Burlesque* with the help of famed dance producer Arthur Baker, who had worked with Bruce Springsteen and Cyndi Lauper and suggested Dylan hired him in order to make him sound "a little more contemporary."

The album ranged from rock to ballads, including an acoustic track, with some studio trickery thrown in, and ignited renewed public interest in Dylan's recordings, hitting the US top 40 and missing the UK Top 10 by just one place.

After closing the US Live Aid event in Philadelphia in July 1985 – backed by Stones' guitarists Keith Richards and Ronnie Wood – and issuing his five-album box set *Biograph* (with its 18 unreleased tracks), Dylan spent parts of both 1985 and 1986 in the studio working on the album *Knocked Out Loaded*.

RIGHT Sharing the vocals with Tom Petty.

Eventually recorded in London and produced by The Eurythmics' Dave Stewart, it featured just eight songs, including covers of 'You Wanna Ramble', 'They Killed Him' and 'Precious Memories', along with tracks left off his previous album. 'Brownsville Girl', co-written with playwright Sam Shepard, was an 11-minute track in the best tradition of his earlier epic songs. Even so, the album only just crept into the UK top 40 and failed to chart in America.

Dylan, who had married singer Carolyn Dennis in 1986, was still a major artist for Columbia where Walter Yetnikoff was president of the CBS label division. He recalled hosting a post-concert dinner party for Dylan in New York in the mid-Eighties but at 2am there was no sign of the star. "(Then) just like that he and his entourage walked through the door. I was expecting Bohemian groupies and scruffy musicians. Instead he arrived with his family – his Jewish uncles, Jewish cousins and Jewish mother."

All this came as no surprise to Yetnikoff, who had dealt with artists throughout his long music business career. "As much as you could deal with Dylan, I dealt with him. I understood how hard he worked to protect his mystique. He was entitled," he said. "I saw him as a master poet, master folk rocker, voice of a generation, American icon and a guy who still sold a shitload of records."

Dylan spent much of 1987 touring, firstly in America with The Grateful Dead and then in Europe with members of Tom Petty's band The Heartbreakers. He also went into the studio, cutting the album *Down In The Groove* which, for many, proved he was struggling to be a contemporary 1980s artist. He filled the albums with covers of early songs by Hank Snow, the Stanley Brothers and Wilbert Harrison, plus 'Sally Sue Brown' (released in 1960 by Arthur Alexander), which he recorded with former Clash man Paul Simonon and ex-Sex Pistol Steve Jones.

Down In The Groove was a top 40 hit in the UK but was surpassed in 1989 by the album *Dylan And The Dead*, when Dylan and the band he'd toured with in 1987 got together to record versions of seven Dylan songs including 'Slow Train', 'All Along The Watchtower' and 'Knockin' On Heaven's Door'. The collection returned Dylan to the US top 40 and continued his run of UK top 40 hits.

Dylan's induction into the Rock and Roll Hall of Fame in January 1989 – when Bruce Springsteen told the audience in New York: "Bob freed your mind in the way Elvis freed your body" – followed his decision in 1988 to join George Harrison, Jeff Lynne, Roy Orbison and Tom Petty as a member of The Traveling Wilburys. Their debut album *Volume One* was a US top three hit while the single 'Handle With Care' reached number 21 in the UK.

RIGHT With Ronnie Wood (L) and Keith Richards during US Live Aid.

BELOW Dylan goes down to the river after a difficult decade.

OVERLEAF Four Wilburys (L to R): Dylan, Tom Petty, Jeff Lynne and George Harrison.

Oh Mercy

Despite all the travails and turbulence of the Eighties, Dylan managed to end the most difficult decade of his career with his most successful and most acclaimed album for years.

Oh Mercy was recorded in the spring of 1989 and signaled his first association with U2's producer Daniel Lanois, who recalled his first experience of working with Dylan. "I sat next to him for two months while he wrote the album and it was extraordinary. He keeps chipping away at his verses."

Lanois had been recommended by U2's Bono, and Dylan remembered his meeting with the French-Canadian producer. "Daniel came to see me when we were playing New Orleans and … we hit it off. He had an understanding of what my music was all about." Getting together with Lanois also enabled Dylan to experience the producer's portable studio, set up in an old colonial house in New Orleans where he was recording The Neville Brothers' album *Yellow Moon*, which featured Dylan's 'Ballad of Hollis Brown' and 'With God On Our Side'.

Taken with the idea of recording in New Orleans, Dylan returned to the city in the spring of 1989 armed with half a dozen songs which dated back to late 1987 and early 1988. Apparently he had shown some of them to George Harrison during The Travelin' Wilburys' sessions and the ex-Beatle urged Dylan to write more and then record them.

The studio in New Orleans was located in a building with, according to Lanois, "a bordello overtone" which was enhanced with moss, stuffed animals and alligator heads. Reluctant to use his touring band, Dylan relied on his new producer to recruit local musicians such as guitarists Mason Ruffner and Brian Stoltz, bassist Tony Hall and drummer Willie Green, while Lanois added dobro, guitar and pedal steel and engineer Malcolm Burn joined in on tambourine, keyboards and bass.

The ten songs that finally made it on to *Oh Mercy* were initially recorded during March and April 1989, before Dylan headed off on another trip to Europe: but before he left the first signs of tension between artist and producer had begun to appear.

Different versions of songs were recorded and discarded, while a local zydeco band were hired but eventually rejected and at one point Dylan despaired over Lanois' treatment of a song called 'Dignity', which missed the album's final track listing. "Whatever promise Dan had seen in the song was beaten into a bloody mess," he said.

During the recording sessions Dylan was also busy writing more songs, and by the end of his time in New Orleans he had around 14 or 15 songs recorded and ready for consideration, despite the continuing friction with Lanois. Explaining that he was pretty much set in his ways, Dylan said "There wasn't much chance in changing now. I didn't need to climb the next mountain." Reflecting on the finished album, he said: "There'd been a clashing of spirits at times but nothing that had turned into a bitter or complicated struggle. I can't say if it's the record either of us wanted."

'Man In A Long Black Coat' has its roots deep in America's folk music history, and Dylan has been quick to acknowledge Lanois' role in the recording. "Like Sam Phillips (the founder of Sun Records who discovered and produced Elvis Presley) he likes to push artists to the psychological edge and he'd done that with me but he didn't have to do any of that with this song."

'Everything Is Broken' was first recorded early on in the New Orleans sessions as 'Broken Days' but by April, a month after the first version, Dylan had rewritten it and given it a new title.

"Lanois thought it was a throwaway," recalled Dylan in his autobiography, "but I didn't think it was, but there was only one way to find out, only one way to cut it – one style and with plenty of tremolo. I thought the song did just what it had to do."

The first recording of 'Where Teardrops Fall', according to Dylan, "took about five minutes and it wasn't rehearsed" and featured local musician Rockin' Dopsie and his zydeco band, whose other work on the album had been rejected. Despite later efforts, Dylan returned to the original version for the album and exclaimed: "It was just a three-minute ballad but it made you stand straight up and stay right where you were. The song was beautiful and magical, upbeat and it was complete."

The final version of *Oh Mercy* was released in September 1989 and restored Dylan to the US top 30 for the first time since 1980, while in the UK, after six low chart entries, Dylan found himself back in the Top 10, at number six.

Oh Mercy
Released 1989. Tracks: Political World / Where Teardrops Fall / Everything Is Broken / Ring Them Bells / Man In The Long Black Coat / Most Of The Time / What Good Am I? Disease Of Conceit / What Was It You Wanted / Shooting Star.

LEFT Dylan adopts a Mexican look for a new decade of touring and recording.

TOP RIGHT Another year older and another new image.

CENTRE RIGHT Dylan hits Rotterdam in Holland during a European tour.

BOTTOM RIGHT Backstage pass from 1989 tour.

"I saw him as a master poet, master folk rocker, voice of a generation, American icon ... and a guy who still sold a shitload of records."

President of Columbia records, Walter Yetnikoff, 1986

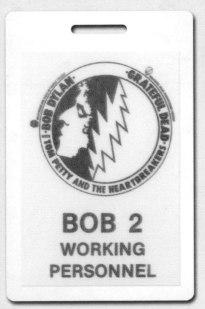

LEFT Dylan and The Grateful Dead join up during a US tour.

ABOVE Bob Dylan, Grateful Dead and Tom Petty concert series backstage pass, 1986.

Into the 1990s

In the wake of *Oh Mercy* Dylan opened the new decade with a festival in Brazil plus guest spots at a Roy Orbison tribute for the homeless, with Bruce Springsteen and Tom Petty and finally alongside Bono, Van Morrison and Nina Simone on various European dates.

He also went back into the studio in spring 1990 to start new album *Under The Red Sky*. Lanois was replaced as producer by Don and David Was, plus Dylan himself (under the name Jack Frost), and they were joined by the largest array of superstars Dylan had ever assembled – George Harrison, Elton John, Slash from Guns N'Roses, Stevie Ray Vaughan, David Crosby and Bruce Hornsby.

For some reason Dylan took to wearing a hooded sweatshirt throughout recording, which left a lasting impression on Slash. "I finally met this guy who looked like an Eskimo … he's wearing a heavy wool sweater with a hood and baseball cap underneath," he said before adding: "He was really impolite. I didn't really have a good time."

In 2006, Dylan explained the album was a hurried affair interrupted by his Traveling Wilburys work, and there were too many people in the studio. It was dedicated to "Gabby Goo Goo," which it transpired was Dylan's nickname for his four-year-old daughter.

Two songs, 'Born In Time' and 'God Knows', were left over from the *Oh Mercy* sessions while 'TV Talkin' Song' was inspired by a visit to Speakers' Corner in London's Hyde Park. Harrison appeared on the title track, while Slash provided guitar on 'Wiggle Wiggle' and John piano on 'Two By Two'.

The album peaked at a disappointing number 38 in the US but a healthier number 13 in the UK.

Having been recognized in France in 1990 by being made a Commandeur de l'Ordre des Arts et des Lettres, and with a Lifetime Achievement award at the 1991 Grammy Awards, Dylan celebrated his own 30th year in the record business with a concert at New York's Madison Square Garden in October 1992, featuring the likes of Harrison, Petty, Eric Clapton, Johnny Cash, Stevie Wonder, Richie Havens and Willie Nelson.

Reflecting on his career the year before, Dylan had said: "Maybe a person gets to the point where they've written enough songs," but it didn't stop him returning to the studio in summer 1992 to embark on a new album, but this time without any original Dylan songs. *Good As I Been To You* emerged from a set of acoustic folk recordings made with David Bromberg as producer, which Dylan scrapped but later re-worked with producer Debbie Gold in his Malibu garage studio.

ABOVE In Spain in 1991 and Dylan plays duelling guitars with Keith Richards of the Rolling Stones.

> **Under The Red Sky**
>
> Released 1990. Tracks: Wiggle Wiggle / Under The Red Sky / Unbelievable / Born In Time
> TV Talkin' Song / 10,000 Men / Two By Two / God Knows / Handy Dandy / Cat's In The Well

Dylan was the only musician credited – on vocals, guitar and harmonica – and he focused on recording a number of traditional songs, including the opening track 'Frankie and Albert', his own version of a Mississippi John Hurt song previously covered by Jerry Lee Lewis and Gene Vincent, and 'Tomorrow Night', which had been recorded by Elvis Presley and Lonnie Johnson.

Credited as arranger on all 13 tracks, Dylan also offered up 'Diamond Joe', a Western ballad covered by his old Sixties folk friends Ramblin' Jack Elliott and Tom Rush, and 'Black Jack Davey', which he was taped singing in 1961. He finished up with a glorious six-minute version of the children's favourite 'Froggie Went A-Courtin'.

Dylan described the songs on the album, which reached number 51 in America and crept into the UK top 20 – as "the music that's true to me."

Before he began work on his next album Dylan continued with his extraordinary round of live work, which took in numerous guest appearances including joining Willie Nelson on stage and on his *Across The Borderline* album, in addition to visiting the UK (again) for a week of shows and debuting at the New Orleans Jazz and Heritage Festival.

He returned to the studio in his Malibu home in May 1993 to record a second collection of traditional folk songs, which he performed acoustically on guitar and harmonica and also produced. In fact, he recorded a total of 14 songs in a matter of a few days and focused on simple and often basic recording techniques in an effort to retain an authentic feel on *World Gone Wrong*.

It featured songs like 'Ragged and Dirty', recorded by Sleepy John Estes in the 1920s and later by Willie Brown, and 'Broke Down Engine', which came from Blind Willie McTell. Title track 'World Gone Wrong' was inspired by a 1930s version by the Mississippi Sheiks, 'Delia' was a song about a murder, which Dylan performed in Minneapolis when he was working the Dinkytown folk clubs, while 'Stack A Lee' dated back to 1928 and Cliff Edwards.

The album, which featured a cover photograph taken in a restaurant in London's Camden Town, gained a modest number 70 placing in the US and a disappointing number 35 in the UK, although it did earn him a Grammy for Best Traditional Folk Album.

Good As I Been To You
Released 1992. Tracks: Frankie and Albert / Jim Jones Black Jack Davey / Canadee-I-O / Sittin' On Top Of The World Little Maggie / Hard Times / Step It Up And Go / Tomorrow Night / Arthur McBride / You're Gonna Quit Me / Diamond Joe / Froggie Went A-Courtin'

ABOVE Dressing in contemporary youth style (**LEFT**) and Dylan collected his French cultural medal in Paris in 1990 (**RIGHT**).

BELOW A rare ticket for The Supper Club concerts, 1993.

OVERLEAF Dave Stewart and Bob Dylan sign autographs for passing fans in Camden, London, 1993.

World Gone Wrong
Released 1993. Tracks: World Gone Wrong / Love Henry / Ragged and Dirty / Blood In My Eyes / Broke Down Engine Delia / Stack A Lee / Two Soldiers / Jack-A-Roe Lone Pilgrim

'02037

Bob Dylan

The Supper Club

240 West 47th Street
Between 8th and Broadway
Showtime 1 a.m.
Doors Open at 10 p.m.

Downstairs

Wednesday, November 17, 1993

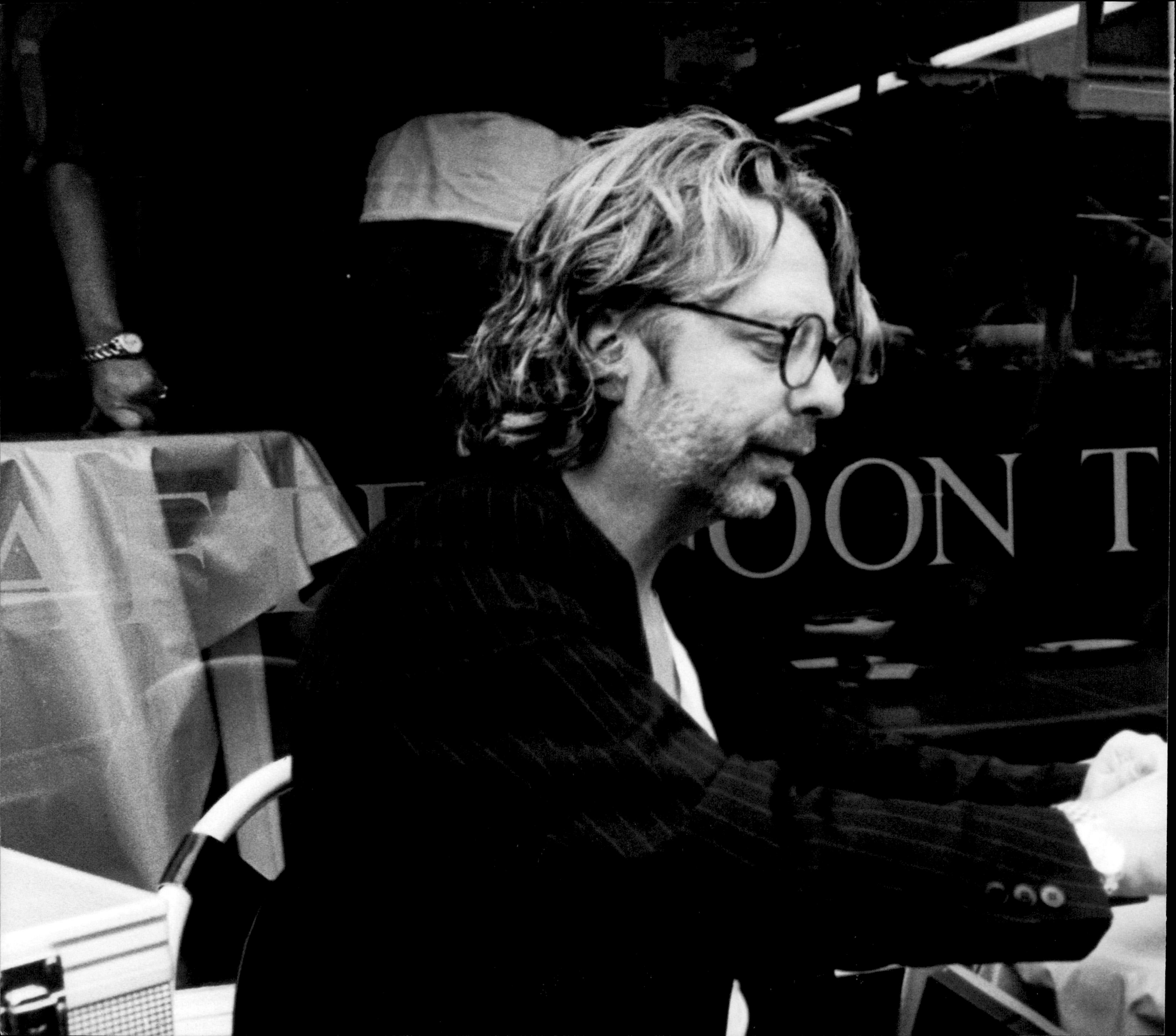

A Return to Form

Dylan's obsession with performing live may have taken the edge off his interest in recording an album of new material. In 1991, after he released *Under The Red Sky*, his last album of new material, Dylan admitted in an interview: "There was a time when songs would come three or four at the same time but those days are long gone."

After his two albums of traditional American folk music, Dylan went back on the road for his own dates and also continued with his habit of duetting along the way; he sang with The Rolling Stones and Bruce Springsteen, and even performed 'Restless Farewell' at a celebration for Frank Sinatra's 80th birthday.

One other date that stood out in his itinerary was the so-called Woodstock II festival, held in August 1994 to mark the 25th anniversary of the original event which Dylan had ignored. This time he travelled to a new site on Winston Farm in Saugerties, New York, to play a 12-song, 78- minute set in front of 250,000 people for a reported fee of $600,000.

In 1996 news filtered through that Dylan was busy on his farm in Minnesota writing a fresh set of songs and in January 1997, when he entered the Criteria Studios in Miami, Florida, to begin recording officially, the producer chosen to work on his 30th studio album was Daniel Lanois, the man behind the hit title *Oh Mercy*.

The musicians assembled for the album included slide guitarist Cindy Cashdollar, drummers Brian Blade and Jim Keltner, guitarists Bob Britt and Duke Robillard plus pianist Jim Dickinson and former Sir Douglas Quintet organist Augie Meyers, while Dylan (again using the name Jack Frost) acted as co-producer on the 11 new songs he chose for the double album.

However, it seems relations between artist and producer were once again pushed to the limit as the band recorded the album live in the studio, with Dylan apparently re-working and editing songs as he went along. Lanois later commented: "Well, you never know what you're going to get. He's an eccentric man," while pianist Dickinson recalled: "Twelve musicians playing live – three sets of drums … it was unbelievable – two pedal steels." He later added that at the end of the album even the musicians weren't sure "who's playing what".

Auger's ghostly organ sound was predominant on the album's opening track 'Love Sick', together with Dylan's slightly unworldly

RIGHT Bob Dylan takes to the stage sporting some fancy embroidery and a cowboy hat.

vocal. He later explained: "It's a spooky record because I feel spooky," and then agreed to it being used in a TV advert for the lingerie store Victoria's Secret (featuring his image and some scantily clad models), while 'Tryin' To Get To Heaven' was a step on from his classic 'Knockin' On' Heaven's Door', and bizarrely hinted at events that would occur later in the year.

According to the revered singer Emmylou Harris, the song 'Not Dark Yet' is the finest work ever written about growing old. "For those of us entering that door, it brings up things we didn't know we were capable of feeling", she said after the album was released.

Not for the first time, Dylan finished the album with the longest track available, and the 16-minute epic 'Highlands' again has a sense of fatality about it with Dylan's eerie commentary namechecking the likes of Erica Jong and Neil Young.

After the completion of the album *Time Out Of Mind* in January 1997 and before its eventual release in September, Dylan fell seriously ill with a heart disorder caused by a fungal infection. He was taken into hospital in the last week of May 1997 and, after a week long stay, was sent home to rest for six months. "I really thought I'd be seeing Elvis soon," was his observation.

By the time the album came out, however, he was back on the road – during the following year he would play 133 live shows – and reflected on *Time Out Of Mind* to *Guitar World* in 1999: "It doesn't take itself seriously, but then again the sound is very significant to that record. There wasn't any wasted effort on *Time Out Of Mind*." The critics were also impressed with the album's sound, *NME* declaring: "The original is back," while *The Guardian* decided he was "at his creative peak" and *Newsweek* magazine ran the headline "Dylan lives", and featured him on the front cover for the first time in 23 years.

While single releases 'Not Dark Yet' and 'Love Sick' failed to make any real impression, *Time Out Of Mind* reached number 10 in both the US (where it was certified platinum) and the UK. It also brought him his best haul of Grammy Awards, being voted Album of the Year and Best Contemporary Folk Album while the song 'Cold Irons Bound' was rated Best Male Rock Vocal Performance. The ceremony in January 1998 became a family affair when Dylan's son Jakob and his band Wallflowers won two Grammys for Best Rock Song and Best Rock Performance by a Group.

Time Out Of Mind
Released 1997. Tracks: Love Sick / Dirt Road Blues / Standing In The Doorway / Million Miles / Tryin' To Get To Heaven / 'Til I Fell In Love With You / Not Dark Yet / Cold Irons Bound / Make You Feel My Love / Can't Wait / Highlands

ABOVE RIGHT Together with Bruce 'The Boss' Springsteen at the Rock And Roll Hall of Fame in 1995.

RIGHT Dylan was joined on stage at the 1998 Grammy Awards by protesting dancer Michael Portnay.

Love and Theft and *Modern Times*

Between albums Dylan was once again on the road, this time sharing the bill with Van Morrison, stepping out as support for The Rolling Stones, touring the US with both Morrison and Joni Mitchell, making his debut at Glastonbury, performing in Australia with Patti Smith and playing nearly 50 shows across America with Paul Simon.

Somewhere along the way he also penned a new song, 'Things Have Changed', for the soundtrack to the film *Wonder Boys*, starring Michael Douglas. In 2001 it won the Oscar for Best Song and he told *The Times*: "A lot of performers have won Grammys but very few have won Academy Awards, so that puts me on a different plateau."

On May 24, 2001, his 60th birthday, Dylan was in the studio in New York working on a new album with his regular backing band of Larry Campbell (guitar/violin/banjo), Charlie Sexton (guitar), Tony Garnier (bass) and David Kemper (drums), plus organist and accordionist Augie Meyers. Again under the name Jack Frost, Dylan produced the *Love and Theft* album, completed between May 9 and 26 and described by Dylan as "autobiographical on every front."

Opening track 'Tweedle Dee and Tweedle Dum' has its heart in the Mardi Gras carnivals of New Orleans and features Clay Meyers on bongos. It's followed by 'Mississippi', a song Dylan offered to Sheryl Crow, who recorded it in 1998 before Dylan, having left it off *Time Out Of Mind*, decided to revisit the song.

'High Water (For Charley Patton)' was a tribute to the legendary Delta blues singer who grew up alongside Leadbelly and Robert Johnson and inspired Dylan. He had used Patton's songs on earlier albums and this song refers directly to Patton's 1929 recording 'High Water Everywhere' about the Mississippi floods of 1927.

Love and Theft was unforgettably released on September 11, 2001 – the day of the terrorist attacks on the World Trade Center in New York and the Pentagon in Washington D.C. – and received an array of five-star reviews, reaching number five in the US and number three in the UK.

After *Love and Theft* the world had to wait a further five years for the next instalment in Dylan's recording career. But while he continued on his merry way around America, Europe and Asia,

ABOVE The musician entertaining, circa 2006.

RIGHT On stage in Denmark as the Dylan traveling show hit Europe in 2001.

Love and Theft
Released September 2001. Tracks: Tweedle Dee and Tweedle Dum / Mississippi / Summer Days / Bye And Bye / Lonesome Day Blues / Floater (Too Much To Ask) / High Water (For Charley Patton) / Moonlight / Honest With Me / Po' Boy / Cry A While / Sugar Baby

he was also putting the finishing touches to the first volume of his autobiography, watching 15 of his albums being remastered and reissued and also hosting his own *Theme Time* radio show.

Early in 2006 he assembled his touring band – regular bass player Garnier was now joined by drummer George G. Receli, guitarists Stu Kimball and Denny Freeman, plus Donnie Herron on steel guitar, violin and mandolin – for a series of rehearsals in the Bardavon 1869 Opera House in Poughkeepsie, New York. Before the end of February, they transferred to Clinton Studios in Manhattan to start and finish the album *Modern Times* in less than three weeks with Dylan again producing as Jack Frost.

While the ten songs were all credited as Dylan originals, there was controversy over the origins of some. The opening track 'Thunder On the Mountain' was alleged to contain a second verse based on Ma Rainey's song 'Memphis Minnie', although Dylan bizarrely replaced the reference to Ma Rainey with a namecheck for Alicia Keys.

It was followed by the blues standard 'Rollin' And Tumblin'' – recorded by Hambone Willie Newbern and Muddy Waters, who has also been credited with composing the song – with new Dylan lyrics after the original first verse.

'Workingman's Blues #2' can be traced to songs by jazz singer June Christy ('June's Blues'), Willie Dixon ('Down In the Bottom') and Big Joe Williams ('Meet Me Around The Corner').

Talking to *Los Angeles Times* writer Robert Hilburn, he appeared unconcerned by the furore over his use of old songs. "I'll take a song I know and simply start playing it in my head. That's the way I meditate," he said. "I'm listening to a song in my head. At a certain point, some words will change and I'll start writing a new song." In 1999, he told *Guitar World*: "I've got 500, 600, 700 songs. I don't have a problem with the backlog of songs. Some fade away and diminish in time and others take their place."

Modern Times

Released 2006. Tracks:
Thunder On the Mountain
/ Spirit On The Water
/ Rollin' And Tumblin'
/ When the Deal Goes
Down / Someday Baby /
Workingman's Blues #2
/ Beyond The Horizon /
Nettie Moore The Levee's
Gonna Break/ Ain't Talkin'

Whether the songs on *Modern Times* were old or new, Dylan originals or adaptations seems to have made no difference to his fans or the critics, who gave it five-star reviews. *Modern Times* became Dylan's first US number one since *Desire* in 1976 and earned him the distinction, at 65, of being the oldest living artist to enter the chart in the top spot. Despite hitting number one in Canada, Australia, Denmark and Norway, it peaked at number three in the UK but passed the six million sales mark worldwide.

Placed at number one in *Rolling Stone* magazine's list of the 50 Greatest Albums of 2006, *Modern Times* also brought Dylan two more Grammys: for Best Contemporary Folk/Americana Album and Best Rock Vocal Performance for 'Someday Baby'.

BELOW Dylan toured the US and Europe with Irish singer Van Morrison.

BOTTOM Backstage pass from the Bob Dylan/Van Morrison tour.

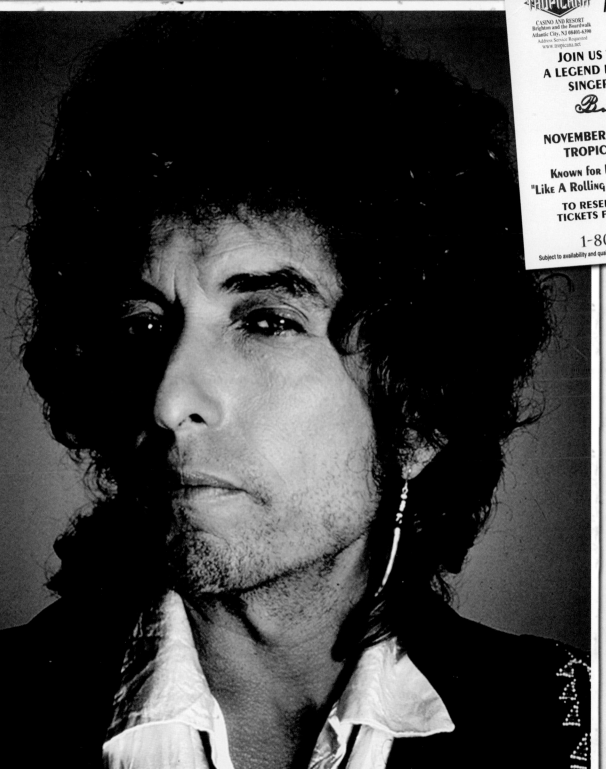

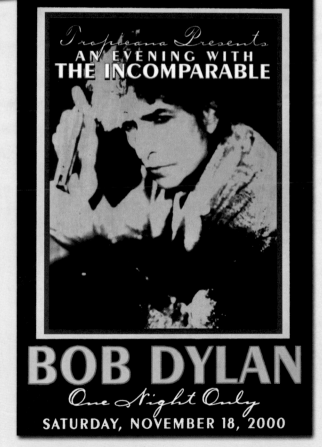

Tropicana Presents
AN EVENING WITH
THE INCOMPARABLE

BOB DYLAN
One Night Only
SATURDAY, NOVEMBER 18, 2000

ABOVE Invite to 'An Evening With Bob Dylan', 2000.

LEFT A stunning portrait of Dylan, in reflective pose.

OPPOSITE He appeared at the 2010 Academy Awards via satellite link from Sydney, Australia.

Together Through Life and Christmas in the Heart

In the three years between the award-winning *Modern Times* and his next studio venture, Dylan spent time on his farm in Minnesota, at his Malibu house in California, and in a host of hotel rooms as he continued in his role as the wandering minstrel.

By the time he returned to recording, he had found a new songwriting partner in The Grateful Dead's lyricist Robert Hunter. They had collaborated on two tracks on Dylan's largely ignored 1988 album *Down In The Groove* and this new partnership represented Dylan's first major co-writing exercise since Jacques Levy and *Desire*.

As the album *Together Through Life* began to evolve in December 2008, Dylan recruited The Heartbreakers' guitarist/mandolin player Mike Campbell and guitarist/accordionist David Hildago (from Los Lobos) to join regular band members Garnier (bass), Recile (drums) and Herron (steel guitar/banjo/trumpet). As Jack Frost, he was still in charge of production duties as the ten tracks took shape.

It seems Dylan's inspiration to make a new album was French film director Olivier Dahan, who asked him to contribute to his movie *My Own Love Song*. Dylan came up with a song, but recalled: "The record sort of took its own direction" after Dahan asked for a whole soundtrack. Dylan also spoke about Hunter, saying: "We could probably write a hundred songs together if we thought it was important or the right reasons were there… He's got a way with words and I do too."

As it was, the pair wrote eight of the album's ten songs, with Dylan adding to Willie Dixon's 'My Wife's Home Town' while 'This Dream Of You' was his only solo song on the album. It was released in April 2009 with little fanfare or advance publicity. Anticipating the reaction, coming as it did after his number one, Grammy-winning *Modern Times*, Dylan reported on his website: "I know my fans will like it. Other than that I have no idea."

He quickly found out the critics were also impressed, one BBC commentator calling it "a masterful reading of 20th-century American folk" while *Mojo* magazine assessed it as "dark yet comforting." Others too gave it a five-star rating, and the fans made *Together Through Life* Dylan's second successive US number one

Together Through Life
Released 2009. Tracks: Beyond Here Lies Nothin' / Life Is Hard / My Wife's Home Town / If You Ever Go To Houston / Forgetful Heart / Jolene / This Dream Of You / Shake Shake Mama I Feel a Change Comin' On / It's All Good

RIGHT Dylan hits all the right notes during one of his 2009 live shows.

album while in the UK it earned him the top spot for the first time since 1970's *New Morning*.

Having recorded protest songs, love songs, folk songs and children's songs, it was still a surprise when Dylan produced a collection of traditional Christmas songs, even if it was to aid charities, with royalties going to Feed America, the United Nations' World Food Programme and Crisis in the UK.

Some time in May 2009 Dylan assembled regulars Garnier, Herron and Recile from his touring band and added Hildago plus guitarist Phil Upchurch, keyboard player Patrick Warren and seven backing singers. With Jack Frost leading the gang, they assembled in Jackson Browne's studio in Santa Monica, California, to bring to life a collection of 15 hymns, carols and seasonal standards.

Although Jewish by birth, Dylan explained, Christmas was "so worldwide and everybody can relate to it in their own way." Asked why he performed them straight, without any of his usual quirkiness, he said: "There wasn't any other way to play it. These songs are part of my life, just like folk songs."

With tracks ranging from 'Winter Wonderland' (a 1957 hit for Johnny Mathis), 'Little Drummer Boy' (recorded by David Bowie with Bing Crosby in 1982) and 'Have Yourself A Merry Little Christmas' (made famous by Judy Garland in 1944 and Frank Sinatra in 1957) to 'Hark The Herald Angels Sing' and

'O Come All Ye Faithful' plus 'O' Little Town of Bethlehem' and 'Here Comes Santa Claus', *Christmas in the Heart* was a delightful enigma to most people.

A BBC review suggested fans "indulge Dylan's whims" as the record was "worth a spin come Christmas morn," while Richard Williams in *The Guardian* noted: "The result is polished without being glib and sympathetic listeners may find it addictive," before adding: "It seems safe to say, however, that no one has ever tackled 'O Come All Ye Faithful' quite like this."

To support the album's release in October 2009, Dylan even made a video for the single 'Must Be Santa', in which he portrayed a Father Christmas character – half Dickensian, half punk – at a seasonal house party which erupts into fighting and mayhem. It made it to number 41 in the UK.

Christmas in the Heart topped both Billboard's US Holiday and Folk album charts while peaking at 23 in the overall chart and reaching number ten in the UK. Significantly, Dylan signed off an interview by saying: "Even at this point in time they (the critics) still don't know what to make of me."

Christmas in the Heart

Released 2009. Tracks: Here Comes Santa Claus / Do You Hear What I Hear? / Winter Wonderland / Hark The Herald Angels Sing I'll Be Home For Christmas / Little Drummer Boy / The Christmas Blues / O Come, All Ye Faithful / Have Yourself A Merry Little Christmas / Must Be Santa / Silver Bells / The First Noel Christmas Island / The Christmas Song / O Little Town Of Bethlehem

RIGHT Nearly 70 years old and still in the spotlight.

BELOW In 2010 Dylan took his Never Ending Tour to Japan, South Korea, Europe and the US.

The Never Ending Tour

Dylan spent the month before his 71st birthday (May 24, 2012) playing dates in Brazil, Argentina and Chile. It was just another leg of what has been dubbed the "Never Ending Tour," although the man himself questions the title, asking: "Does anybody call Henry Ford a never-ending car builder?"

By all accounts the "NET" started with a concert in the Pavilion in Concord, California, on June 7, 1988, and the 20th and 21st centuries' ultimate troubadour has been circling the globe ever since. The roots of the longest tour in rock history lie in Dylan's association with The Grateful Dead and their philosophy that music is all about playing live rather than recording – something Dylan took on board after he played with The Dead in early 1988.

Averaging more than 100 dates a year, regularly taking in America, Canada, Europe, Japan, Australia, New Zealand and South America – he included Israel, China and South-East Asia in 2011 – Dylan explained: "I knew I've got to go out and play these songs. You just don't have to start it up and end it. It's better just to keep it out there."

Once he got over his less than enthusiastic reception in 1966, Dylan maintained a healthy relationship with the UK, regularly including it in his itinerary between 1978 and 1987, the year before the "NET" began, when CBS UK chairman Paul Russell faced a particular challenge.

"He was playing Wembley and we had a platinum disc that I wanted to give to him," says Russell. "We put together a small gathering of around 20 people – top retailers, top broadcasters who had helped his career – and invited them to come backstage."

However, when Russell was told Dylan wouldn't attend the presentation, he was forced into action. "We'd invited these people so it was difficult to cancel. I went to Wembley early on the day of the show and spoke to Dylan's manager, who said: 'He doesn't do presentations'. I said I wanted to see Bob to talk about it and the manager said: 'He's in that room down there with a couple of his mates so why don't you go and talk to him? Good luck'."

Russell knocked and went in. "There was Bob with Ringo Starr and George Harrison. I explained why I was there and said it'd take him 30 seconds to take the disc and have a photo taken. He said: 'I don't want to do it. I don't do record presentations'. Then Ringo said: 'Bob, don't be a c**t – everybody has to do these things', and Bob looked over at George, who just said that it went with the territory.

"So Bob did it. He walked in, put his arm round my shoulder, didn't even touch the disc, had his picture taken and then walked out the door. And I've still got the picture," says Russell, proudly.

While Simply Red's Mick Hucknall appreciates Dylan's influence on a generation of rock musicians, he has deliberately avoided seeing him live. "I've never seen him in concert. I hear nothing but bad reviews so I've never actually bothered because I didn't want to be disappointed."

On the other hand, Cockney Rebel leader Steve Harley, who covered Dylan's 'Love Minus Zero/No Limit' on his 1996 album *Poetic Justice*, waited until the mid-Nineties before going to see the man who "changed my whole outlook on life in early 1963. I was inspired by the imagery of his songs – it grabbed me."

At the Phoenix Festival in Stratford-on-Avon in 1995, Harley had his own close-up moment. A backstage guest, he was in the hospitality marquee after watching Dylan's performance from the wings – "It's never the best place to see a show but it was a privilege" – when Dylan and his band wandered in.

"He was in his espadrilles and his hoodie, and when they got up to leave Bob was at the back of the line, just at my shoulder.

I thought: 'I can't let this moment go', and, as Dylan had changed my life since the age of 12, why would I let this moment go without saying something?

"I stood up and put my hand out. He looked at me and I said: 'Hi; I'm Steve Harley', and he said 'Hey, man' – it was recognition. He sat with me and my two pals, kept his head down, just nodding every now and again but saying nothing. It wasn't a conversation and after ten minutes I was running out of things to say.

"He'd had enough and was getting up to leave when I said something about the heavy rain that was falling and that it was a good job he didn't have to play his set in the rain. He looked at me – for the second time – and just said 'The weather, the weather', and walked off."

By the end of 2011 Dylan and his band had completed close to 2,500 shows on the "Never Ending Tour" with, according to a fan's log, 'Mr Tambourine Man' the most performed song, followed by 'Highway 61 Revisited' and 'Tangled Up In Blue'.

While some performances have been described as "unpredictable" and his lyrics as "effectively unrecognizable", Dylan has shown no sign of ending his gigantic jaunt around the world but he once told the *LA Times*: "I could stop any time … I can see an end to everything, really."

BELOW A rare photo of Dylan at a disc presentation by Paul Russell of CBS/Sony in 1987.

OPPOSITE and RIGHT "Better just to keep it out there" is Dylan's motto as the show rolls on.

OVERLEAF Some fancy head gear for Dylan and his band members during their 2010 tour.

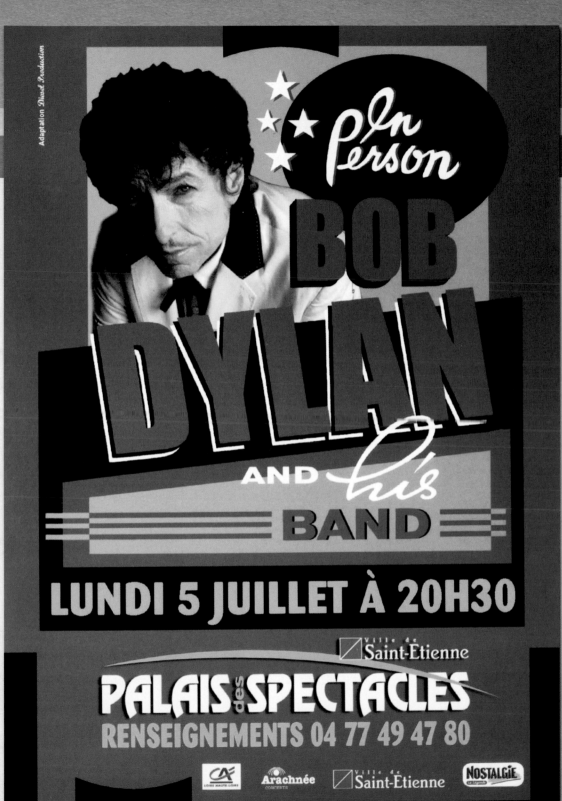

SWEET MARIE
SENOR/TONIGHT I'L BE STAYING
TOUGH MAMA
TEARS OF RAGE/JUST LIKE A WOMAN
SILVIO
────────
TAMBOURINE/RAMONA (STEEL)
TANGLED/MASTERS
COCAINE
────────
RIVER FLOW
BLIND WILLIE MC TELL
TOMBSTONE BLUES/HIGHWAY/PILLBOX
────────
ROLLING STONE
BACK PAGES

ABOVE Bob Dylan original setlist. 'Mr Tambourine Man' and 'Tangled Up In Blue' are the two most songs played on Dylan's Never Ending tour.

LEFT Promo flyer for Dylan's concert in St Etienne, France, 2004.

OPPOSITE The Man in the Shadows still plays over 100 shows a year. "I could stop anytime," he famously once said.

Acknowledgements

In addition to the titles listed below, the author also visited back issues of *Melody Maker*, *New Musical Express* and *Rolling Stone* (all courtesy of the British Library) and acknowledges a debt of thanks to all those who wrote the words way back when, plus all the people who gave up their time to speak to me … both on and off the record.

Brits And Bobs: Bob Dylan In The British Isles – Steve Butterworth (Eye 5 2003)

Chronicles, Volume One – Bob Dylan (Simon & Schuster 2004)

Dylan On Dylan – The Essential Interviews (Hodder 2007)

Howling At The Moon – Walter Yetnikoff (Abacus 2004)

Life: Keith Richards – Keith Richards (Phoenix 2011)

Who Are You : The Life of Pete Townshend – Mark Wilkerson (Omnibus 2008)

Revolution In The Air: The Songs of Bob Dylan 1957–73 – Clinton Heylin (Constable 2009)

Still On The Road: Songs of Bob Dylan 1974–2008 – Clinton Heylin (Constable 2010)

The Rough Guide To Bob Dylan – Nigel Williamson (Rough Guides 2004)

RIGHT Bob Dylan, in the mid-1980s, contemplates his future. "Maybe a person gets to the point where they've written enough songs?"; Further groundbreaking success was just around the corner.

OPPOSITE A flyer advertising the Bob Dylan and Paul Simon Hollywood Bowl concert of June 22, 1999'; "Never heard of him," was Dylan's first thoughts on Simon.

"There was nothing easy going about the folk songs I sang. They weren't friendly or ripe with mellowness. They didn't come gently to the shore. I guess you could say they weren't commercial."

Bob Dylan, 2004

Picture credits

The publishers would like to thank the following sources for their kind permission to reproduce the photographs in this book.

Key: t = top, b = bottom, l = left, r = right and c = centre

Corbis: /Alesandra Benedetti: 90r

Rudi Daugsch: 9bc

Getty Images: 6-7, 8 (x4), 11 (x4), 20r, 33l, 65r, 85r, 91br; /Buzzfoto/FilmMagic: 81tr; /Redferns: 9br, 12l, 12r, 13tr, 13bc, 14, 15bl, 21r, 33br, 36-37, 40, 41l, 41r, 42l, 42r, 43r, 48, 49r, 53tr, 59l, 62r, 63r, 68, 72r, 80, 81br, 82l, 83l, 83r, 85l, 88l, 89r, 95; /Michael Ochs Archive: 24-25bc, 29br, 32bl, 34bc, 43l, 46cr, 54l, 69, 70, 72l, 73b, 74-75, 86-87; /Time & Life Pictures: 15tr, 16-17, 23tl, 23tr, 56-57, 77l, 79l, 81bl; /Wireimage: 55tr, 77r, 91c

© Bob Gruen: 34r, 52l, 53r, 59br, 66-67

The Kobal Collection: /Starmavale/Swan Song: 65l

Bob Masse: 9bl, 33tr

Mirrorpix: 15br

Ikumi Numata: 44l, 44-45, 49br

Press Association Images: /AP Photo: 90bl; /Suzan: 91tr

Private Collection: 9tr, 18, 22, 28, 58, 84, 91b

Photoshot: /Michael Putland/Retna: 19, 26-27, 46br, 52r, 62l, 64r, 76bl; /Peter Mazel/Sunshine/Retna: 53c; /Retna Pictures: 89bc; /Sunshine/Retna: 76r; /Ronald van Caem/Tolca/Sunshine/Retna: 78-79b; /Chris Walter/Photofeatures/Retna: 24bl, 31, 64bl

Rex Features: /Blake-Ezra Cole: 91cl; /James Fortune: 47t, 47b, 49l, 63l; /Globe Photos Inc.: 4; /Ilpo Musto: 20l, 35, 82r, 88r; /Ray Stevenson: 29tl, 72c; /Richard Young: 21l

Rob Roth/Paul Grushkin: 30l, 38tr, 60-61, 71tl, 71r, 78bl, 96

Tracks: 2, 10, 25t, 30tr, 30br, 32r, 38l, 39, 50tl, 50r, 51, 71bl

Urbanimage.tv: 54r, 55l, 55br, 93; /Adrian Boot: 79c

Frank White Photo Agency: /Ron Aki: 73l

Every effort has been made to acknowledge correctly and contact the source and/or copyright holder of each picture and Carlton Books Limited apologises for any unintentional errors or omissions, which will be corrected in future editions of this book.

LEFT A young Dylan, as many of his legions of devoted fans will no doubt remember him, in Sheridan Square Park, New York in 1965.

RIGHT 'Tambourine Man' poster, complete with classic '60s psychedelia effect.